Basic Urban Disaster Preparedness

Kelly Runer

For Carrie

Table of Contents

Part 1: Getting Started

If you have no idea where to begin, this section is for you:
It'll get you started down your path to preparedness.

- Purpose and Scope
- Basic Preparedness Steps
- Basic Evacuation Steps

Purpose and Scope

If this reference achieves its goal, it will give you, someone living in a city or suburb, enough information to help prevent and prepare for emergencies and disasters. They are not fun to think about, but they happen, and you need to be ready.

This is not an end of the world / run off to a compound in the woods book for extreme survivalists, and if that's what you are looking for, you will have no trouble finding material to meet your needs elsewhere. But if you are reading this to get basic, clearly explained information on how to prevent and survive weather-related or human-caused emergencies, and if you feel a little lost and maybe don't know where to begin, then this reference is geared toward you.

No assumptions are made about your prior training, background, or political leanings. I myself was never a Girl Scout, never in the military—as a matter of fact, I learned because I care passionately about protecting my family, friends, and own skin. There is a wonderful sense of freedom that comes with working toward self-sufficiency and feeling some sense of control in such a chaotic world, no matter who you are.

A scope of about two weeks is covered here. Unless the world really is ending, most emergencies end within that timeframe. Either way, you have to start somewhere, and preparation for two weeks is rational and actually strongly encouraged by our own US government. You may find this scope as adequate to your preparedness needs; if not, use it as a springboard into longer-term preparation.

Basic Preparedness Steps

Many people don't even know where to begin and quickly become overwhelmed. Don't worry: Preventing and preparing for emergencies doesn't take a lot of work or tons of money, unless you let it. You of course get the details for each of these steps in other sections, but here is an overview of the actions you should take and where you can locate the specifics:

- Gather together your emergency preparedness information, what you would find in this reference and in equivalent resources. You want your knowledge easily accessible and portable, preferably in one small book or notebook

- Gather together your supplies for your home, car, and bug out bag. Keep track of what you've bought and what you still need to get (**Part 2**)

- Decide on and practice your evacuation plan (**Part 1**)

- Learn how to shut off your home's utilities: gas, electric, and water. Find out your landlord's wishes if you rent (**Part 1**)

- Prepare your pets for emergencies, including evacuation (**Part 4**)

- Local police department, fire department, and the Poison Control Center—write down and program these numbers into your phones. Also program ICE (In Case of Emergency) contacts into your cell phones (**Part 4**)

- Work toward meeting all prevention tips covered in this book (**PREVENTION** sections)

- Take a CPR/first aid course (through the Red Cross or similar organizations) and stay current with your certification

- Learn how to swim if you can't already (through the Red Cross or similar organizations)

- Work toward meeting the physical and emotional health basics (**Part 6**)

- Practice the techniques covered in the survival priorities sections (**Part 3**, **Part 4**)

- Take a self-defense course

Basic Evacuation Steps

Many emergency situations call for you to evacuate your home, and you may need to do so within minutes. What can you do beforehand to prepare? First of all, put together your family's bug out bags. You will learn how to do so in **Part 2**.

Next, set up four different places in four different directions you can go to in other cities or towns, possibly with close friends or family. Learn secondary roads, not interstates, to those places. Share information about those places with your family. Always keep at least a half tank of gas in your car. If you don't have a car, plan for alternate ways of evacuating.

Come up with communication and evacuation plans for work and school: Make sure everyone in your family knows what to do and where to meet up if they are at those locations and need to evacuate. These meet-up locations should be accessible by foot and easy to locate.

Finally, practice your evacuation plan to streamline the process and make it faster. If authorities tell you to evacuate or your own experience indicates you should do so, remember the following important steps:

- Gather your bug out bags (one for each family member) and any other necessary supplies

- Shut off your gas, electric, and water if you are a homeowner and have the time. Remember that a professional may have to turn your gas back on when you return. If you rent, discuss with your landlord ahead of time and follow their wishes

- Shut off and unplug all appliances if you have the time

- Leave a note indicating where you are going and when you left

- If able, call or email your contact to let them know that you are coming. Keep all phone calls brief

- Lock all doors behind you, and don't forget to take your pets

If you live in a high-rise building, know where your emergency exits are and at least two different exits from the building. Avoid elevators and stay to the right when going down stairwells (in case emergency personnel need to come up).

If you or someone in your family has a disability or special need, be sure to plan ahead for any extra supplies and help needed. Visit www.nod.org or www.ncd.gov for helpful information.

Part 2: Supplies

Having the right supplies for your home, car, and bug out
bags is an important aspect of disaster preparedness, and
gathering the items is a good place to begin.

- For Your Home
- For Your Car
- For Your Bug Out Bag

For Your Home

Some emergencies may require you to evacuate your home, but many call for you to stay put. Disaster agencies like the Red Cross recommend at least a two-week supply of items like water, food, and so on. Remember to include your pets in your planning.

You just can't assume that a city's vital services will be running during an emergency: Gas stations, grocery stores, and so on may be closed or so overwhelmed with panicked citizens as to be useless or even dangerous. In the city during an emergency, other people may be just as dangerous as the situation itself, so it's better to stay home and keep a low profile if you are staying put. Here are recommended items you should have in your home:

Air:
Carbon monoxide detectors
Clear plastic sheeting
Duct tape
Scissors
Gas masks (or N100 particulate masks)
Potassium Iodate (or Potassium Iodide)
Portable air filter (with HEPA filter)

Shelter:
Tent (large enough for whole family)
Sewing kit
Knife (and knife sharpener)
Sunscreen (SPF 15 or higher)
Bug repellant
Rope (50' or longer)
Snow shovel
Rock salt

Basic toolkit (including extra nails)
Sturdy step stool
Extra sleeping bag or warm blanket per person
Extra set of clothing per person (including hat, gloves, shoes, and poncho)

Water:
Water purification system (with backup cartridges)
Coffee filters
Unscented bleach
Medicine dropper
Rain barrel
Large clean tarp
Clean buckets (2 or more)

Set aside the equivalent of one gallon of water per person per day for drinking and sanitation. That means 14 gallons per person to meet the 2+ week minimum amount. Keep around some empty containers that you can quickly fill up as well.

Fire:
Fire alarms
Fire extinguishers
Matches (in airtight container)
Lighters
Firestarter
Axe
Metal shovel
Work gloves
Extra batteries
Alternate light sources:
      LED flashlights
      Battery-powered lamps
      Propane lamps

Kerosene lamps
Solar-powered lamps
Hand-crank lamps and/or
Light sticks
Alternate cooking sources:
Flameless food heaters
Wood stove
Camp stove
Charcoal grill
Sterno and/or
Fireplace
Alternate heating sources:
Catalytic heater
Camp stove
Battery-powered space heater
Chemical hand warmers and/or
Fireplace
Extra fuel:
Wood
Propane
Kerosene and/or
Charcoal

Candles are a major fire hazard and should be avoided.

Food:
Refrigerator thermometer
Meat thermometer
Paper plates and cups
Plastic utensils
Extra paper towels
Aluminum foil
Non-electric can opener
Daily vitamins (2+ week supply)

Store the equivalent of 2+ weeks' worth of non-perishable food for each person. This food shouldn't require any refrigeration, freezing, cooking, or preparation. Avoid foods that take a lot of water to make as well. Here are some suggestions:

Military MREs (Meals Ready to Eat)
Backpacker meals
Energy bars
Dried fruit
Peanuts and peanut butter
Granola
Jerky
Canned tuna
Dry cereal
Crackers
Powdered milk
Canned juices
Baby food (as needed)

Hope:
See **Survival Priorities: Hope** section for suggestions

First Aid:
A complete first aid kit is essential for your home. You can buy prepackaged kits, but it's often cheaper and more comprehensive to put one together yourself. Keep your first aid kit in a cool, dry place that is easily accessible. Keep track of expiration dates. Here are the basic items you should have:

First aid reference material
Immunization and medical history
Disposable gloves
Safety goggles

Ear protection
Bandages (gauze for wounds, elastic for sprains, and triangular for slings)
Sterile wound dressings
Bandaids
Finger splints
Surgical tape
Antiseptic wipes
Rubbing alcohol
Antibiotic ointment (Neosporin, etc.)
Burn ointment (aloe vera gel, etc.)
Eye wash solution (saline, etc.)
Digital thermometer (with plastic covers)
Tweezers
Antihistamine (Benadryl, etc.)
Antacid (Tums, etc.)
Anti-diarrhea medication (Loperamide, etc.)
Pain reliever (Advil, Tylenol, etc.)
Laxative (Ex-Lax, etc.)
Hemorrhoid preparation (Preparation H, etc.)
Cough medicine and cough drops
Hydrocortizone cream (Cortaid, etc.)
Petroleum jelly (Vaseline, etc.)
Ice pack/Heat pack
Prescription medications and supplies (2+ week supply) (as needed)
Extra eyeglasses and/or contact lenses (as needed)

Do not keep syrup of ipecac or activated charcoal in your home: They are no longer recommended for swallowed poisons.

Hygiene/Waste Disposal:
Extra garbage bags
Lidded bucket

Wet wipes
Soap
Hand sanitizer (Purell, etc.)
Disinfectant spray (Lysol, etc.)
Toilet paper (2+ week supply)
Personal toiletry items (2+ week supply)
Extra feminine hygiene supplies (as needed)
Baby diapers (2+ week supply) (as needed)

Communication:
Emergency reference material (like this reference)
Battery-powered or hand-crank radio
Cell phone
Battery-powered or hand-crank cell phone charger
Whistle
Signaling mirror
Emergency flares (at least three)
Binoculars

Defense:
See **Other Priorities: Defense** section for suggestions

Finance:
Cash (at least $100 in small bills and change)
Important documents (See **Supplies: For Your Bug Out Bag** section)
Paper shredder
Fireproof, watertight safe

Navigation:
GPS
Compass
Analog watch
Maps (local, state, and country)

Pets:
Pet food (2+ week supply)
Cat litter (2+ week supply) (as needed)
Scooper
Small plastic bags
Pet medicines (2+ week supply) (as needed)
Transport method
Veterinary records
Collar with identification and rabies tags (as needed)
Leash (as needed)
Pets Inside stickers or signs (one for each entrance)

You may of course add other items to this list, and if you feel the need, you can work to prepare your home for even longer-term situations. Do you want to stock up on firewood, for example? Get a chainsaw? Stockpile certain items for possible bartering? The list above just gets you started.

For Your Car

Here are the basic items you should keep in your car for emergencies:

Shelter:
Blanket
Knife
Extra set of clothes (including hat, gloves, and poncho)

Water:
At least one gallon of water

Fire:
Matches (in airtight container)
Lighters
Metal shovel
Work gloves
Chemical hand warmers
LED flashlight
Spare batteries for flashlight

Food:
Enough to survive at least 12 hours (energy bars, etc.)

First Aid:
Small version of kit found in **Supplies: For Your Home** section

Hygiene/Waste Disposal:
Wet wipes
Garbage bag
Tissues or napkins

Communication:
Cell phone
Car or battery-powered cell phone charger
AAA membership or other emergency service
Proof of car insurance
Proof of car registration
Car owner's manual
Pad of paper and pens
Emergency flares (at least three)
Reflective red triangle

Defense:
See **Other Priorities: Defense** section for suggestions

Finance:
Cash (at least $20 in small bills and change)

Navigation:
GPS
Compass
Maps (local, state, and country)

Transportation:
Extra windshield wiper fluid
Spare tire
Jack
Lug nut wrench (tire iron)
WD-40 or other penetrating oil
Tire pressure gauge
Foam tire sealant
Tire pump
Jumper cables
Snow scraper
Electrical tape
Basic toolkit

Seat belt cutter tool

Remember to regularly replace items that expire.

For Your Bug Out Bag

Your bug out bag, a bag you prepack for hasty evacuation, is essential to good disaster preparation. If you had to leave your home quickly, could you do so in under 10 minutes? Not without planning, of course.

You don't want your bug out bag to be so heavy that you can't carry it for long distances if necessary, but you also need to pack the essentials to live out of your bag for at least 3 days, maybe even longer. Now, you may be tempted to pack your bag and never touch its contents again, but that isn't your best option because some of the items will expire. Plus, you may need to use some of the items and then misplace them.

Here's a better suggestion: Make a list of all the items you want in your bag, and keep that list with your bag. That way, in an emergency when you're probably not thinking of details, you can just check off list items as you quickly gather them. You can of course prepack any items that won't expire.

You will most likely come up with something a little different that works for you, but here is a suggested list of items. Make sure each family member has a bug out bag.

Air:
Gas mask (or N100 particulate masks) (as needed)
Potassium Iodate or Potassium Iodide (as needed)

Shelter:
Blanket or military poncho liner
Pocket-sized emergency blanket
Poncho

Sewing kit
Knife
Knife sharpener
Rope (50' or longer)
Leatherman tool
Sunglasses
Sunscreen (SPF 15 or higher)
Bug repellant
Complete change of clothes
Hat and gloves (as needed)

Water:
Water bottle (preferably with built-in purifier and spare cartridges)
Coffee filters
Water (3+ gallons) (may need to carry in a separate bag)

Fire:
Lighters
Matches (in airtight container)
Firestarter
Axe (fold-up)
Metal shovel (fold-up)
Work gloves
Chemical hand warmers
LED flashlight
Extra batteries (all sizes needed)

Food:
Utensil set
Cup
Small can opener
Flameless food heaters or Sterno (if using MREs or backpacker meals)
Food (3+ day supply)

Seek out food that packs a lot of energy, requires no or little cooking, and doesn't take up space. Suggested items include US military MREs (Meals Ready to Eat), backpacker meals, energy bars, jerky, nuts, powdered protein drinks, dried fruit, and canned tuna.

Hope:
See **Survival Priorities: Hope** section for suggestions

First Aid:
Small version of kit found in **Supplies: For Your Home** section

Hygiene/Waste Disposal:
Wet wipes
Hand sanitizer
Garbage bag(s)
Small plastic bag(s)
Tissues
Camping towel
Personal toiletries (toothbrush, toothpaste, and soap)
Feminine hygiene supplies (as needed)

Communication:
Battery-powered or hand-crank radio
Cell phone
Battery-powered or hand-crank cell phone charger
Pad of paper and pens
Whistle
Signaling mirror
Flares (at least 3)
Emergency reference material (like this reference)

Defense:
See **Other Priorities: Defense** section for suggestions

Finance:
Cash (whatever you can take; include small bills and change)
Fake wallet (to fool robbers)
Important documents in a zipped, waterproof container:

>Flash drive and/or computer backup disk
>Address book
>Pictures of family, closest friends, and pets
>Social security card
>Passport
>Birth certificate
>Car title/registration
>Insurance information
>Banking information
>Utility information

Navigation:
GPS
Compass
Analog watch
Maps (local, state, and country)

Pets (for each):
Collar with identification tag and rabies tag (as needed)
Veterinary records
Pet food (3+ day supply in airtight container)
Water (3+ day supply)
Pet medicines (3+ day supply) (as needed)
Favorite toy
Food and water dishes
Small poop scoop and plastic bags

Transport method (leash, cat carrier, cage, etc.)
Leash (as needed)

If you have pets, your best bet is to make a separate bug out bag for them.

Bug out bags can be made lighter by only having one or two people in your family carry a certain item, like a fold-up shovel, for example. Be careful, though: Most items are essential to each person and should be duplicated in each bag. If you are able to evacuate in a car, you can obviously bring even more with you.

Once you have your bags and items gathered, practice your timing: Were you ready to go in under 10 minutes? That's the timeframe recommended by the U.S. Department of Homeland Security. Obviously some situations, like a fire, could require you to have to leave in seconds.

Part 3: Survival Priorities

You can't live without air, shelter, water, fire, food, or hope. This part addresses each priority in detail after first explaining the all-important Rule of Threes.

- The Rule of Threes and City Vital Services
- Priority One: Air
- Priority Two: Shelter
- Priority Three: Water
- Priority Four: Fire
- Priority Five: Food
- Priority Six: Hope

The Rule of Threes and City Vital Services

Think threes: three minutes without air, three hours without shelter, three days without water, three weeks without food, and three months without hope. Every human is different, of course, but this generalization can help you to remember your survival priorities. Situations are variable, but here are the priorities in their usual order of importance:

Air, Shelter, Water, Fire, Food, Hope

You will of course want to plan beyond this basic list, including the other priorities covered in **Part 4**. Still, you must be able to provide at least these priorities, and applying the Rule of Threes, have at least three completely separate sources for each priority. Have a backup to your backup, in other words. To start a fire, for example, you can have lighters, then matches as your backup, then flint as your backup to your backup. Whatever methods you have to provide for these priorities, they should not be dependent on each other. That way, if one method fails (which often happens in an emergency), you still have your two other methods.

Here's a related basic survival rule: Never put more energy into trying to provide for your survival priorities than you get out of the activity. You will only lower your survival chances. For example, you wouldn't want to expend a lot of energy scrounging in a field for hours just to gather a few berries.

Although cities and suburbs typically provide all your vital services, you have to be prepared to provide for them on your own during an emergency. Some shutdowns may last only hours while others may drag on for weeks or even months. Be ready if and when you lose the following services:

Shelter: gas utility, public building maintenance

Water: water utility

Fire: electric utility, fire department

Food: grocery stores, food pantries, convenience marts

First Aid: hospitals, clinics, pharmacies, dentists

Hygiene/Waste Disposal: garbage collection, sewage

Communication: radio, television, landline phone, cell phone, mail, Internet, libraries, schools, universities, daycare centers

Defense: police department, military, private security

Finance: bank branches, ATMs, check-cashing services

Transportation: gas stations, roadway maintenance, towing services, trucks, buses, cabs, airplanes, ships

Pets: veterinarians, pet stores

Priority One: Air

You won't last very long at all if you can't breathe safely.

PREVENTION: Practicing Carbon Monoxide Safety

Install carbon monoxide detectors near your home's sleeping areas, avoiding corners where air doesn't circulate. Follow the directions carefully on installation and testing, and don't cover detectors with furniture or draperies. The package or manual should state that the alarm meets the IAS 6-96 standard.

To cut down on carbon monoxide in your home, do the following:

- Keep your fireplace flue open when you're using it

- Only burn charcoal outside, never indoors

- Only use portable fuel-burning camping equipment outside, never indoors

- Only use an approved indoor wood-burning stove, and make sure it vents to the outside. It should be approved to meet EPA emission standards

- Use an exhaust fan that vents to the outside over a gas stove, and never use gas appliances for heating your home

- Always turn off gas-powered engines in indoor spaces, like your garage

- Have your heating system inspected and serviced every year

- Always follow directions carefully when servicing your fuel-burning appliances, and get professional help if you're not sure what to do

Protecting Your Airways

Certain emergencies, like a chemical attack, make the air unsafe to breathe. You need a mask to filter out contaminated particles. Full gas masks can be found online and at army/navy outlets and provide the best protection (they are also more expensive). You should follow the directions carefully, practice, and keep the gasmasks in an easily accessible location. Be aware that adult gas masks don't fit well on children.

Your next best option is to invest in N100 or N95 particulate masks, which can be found even in "big box" stores. N100 means it filters out 99.99 percent of harmful particles; N95 means it filters out 95 percent, which is the minimum recommended for most situations, like a pandemic. Again, follow the directions carefully, practice, and keep the masks accessible. Read the directions carefully to see how long you can wear the same mask before it loses effectiveness.

Standard dust masks are cheap and can be found just about anywhere, but they won't protect your airways from airborne diseases or gases. They do provide protection from dust and other airborne particles, though.

Have Potassium Iodate (KI03) or Potassium Iodide (KI) on hand to take if authorities give direction to do so in a nuclear blast or radiation attack (dirty bomb) emergency. Potassium Iodate is preferable to Potassium Iodide because it has less of a health risk and is not as bitter tasting as Potassium Iodide. They will both, however, help protect your thyroid from radiation, but you need to follow the directions on the bottle carefully. Keep track of the expiration date as well. Consider keeping some Potassium Iodate (or Iodide) on you in a small pill fob or other secure container for quick access.

Sheltering in Place

If authorities instruct you to shelter in place, you need to know exactly what they mean: It's more than just staying put in your home or current location. Your best defense in certain emergencies is to evacuate, but that's not always possible. In the event of a biological attack, chemical attack, nuclear blast, or radiation attack (dirty bomb), or when a lot of debris fills the air, you need to make an airtight shelter as quickly as possible to help protect your airways.

- Gather your family and pets to your pre-designated shelter area, such as your basement or an interior room of your house without windows, and stockpile your other emergency supplies there (including a radio, computer, or TV for communication)

- Turn off all air conditioning, heating, and fans

- Close all doors, windows, and fireplace and air vents

- Use clear plastic sheeting, duct tape, and scissors to seal off the room or area as much as possible from outside contaminants. Do this to doorways, windows, fireplaces, air vents, and any other possible access points (It saves time if you've already measured and precut the plastic sheeting)

- Set up and use your portable air filter (with HEPA filter) if you have one

- Don't leave the area until given the all clear by authorities

Remember to protect your airways with gas masks or particulate masks as well.

Priority Two: Shelter

Without shelter from cold, rain, and other elements, you can die within hours. Shelter gives warmth and protection, and it comes in two forms: a protective enclosure and clothing. You must be prepared with both.

PREVENTION: Practicing Sun Safety

Technically, protecting your skin from harmful ultraviolet (UV) rays qualifies as a form of shelter, one that you must think about even on cloudy days. Keep the following basics in mind:

Covering Up: Apply generous amounts of sunscreen to all exposed skin every two hours or after swimming or sweating, and make sure it has a Sun Protection Factor (SPF) of at least 15. Never use old sunscreen because it loses its effectiveness over time. Wear lip balm with sunscreen protection. Cover up as much of your skin as possible with protective clothing, including a hat and sunglasses.

Avoiding Trouble: Don't use tanning beds. Don't get sunburns because they increase your risk for skin cancer. Stick to shady spots as much as possible, especially between 10 am and 4 pm, when the sun's rays are strongest. Be extra careful near water, sand, and snow because they increase your chance of sunburn. Be aware that certain medications raise your risk for sunburn.

Staying Informed: Learn the skin cancer warning signs and get regular skin check-ups. Stay informed of the day's UV Index, which is issued in many larger cities by the National Weather Service: www.nws.noaa.gov.

Treating Sunburn: If you get sunburn, cool the affected area with a cool bath or shower or towel dipped in cold water. Take pain medication, drink plenty of water, and rest in a cool, quiet room. Apply aloe vera gel to the area 2 or 3 times a day. Avoid creams or sprays that numb pain because they can cause allergic reactions. If you have to go out in the sun again, make sure the area is covered.

PREVENTION: Understanding the Wind Chill Factor

The wind chill factor is how cold the temperature really is once wind speed is added to the equation. Use the chart below to calculate:

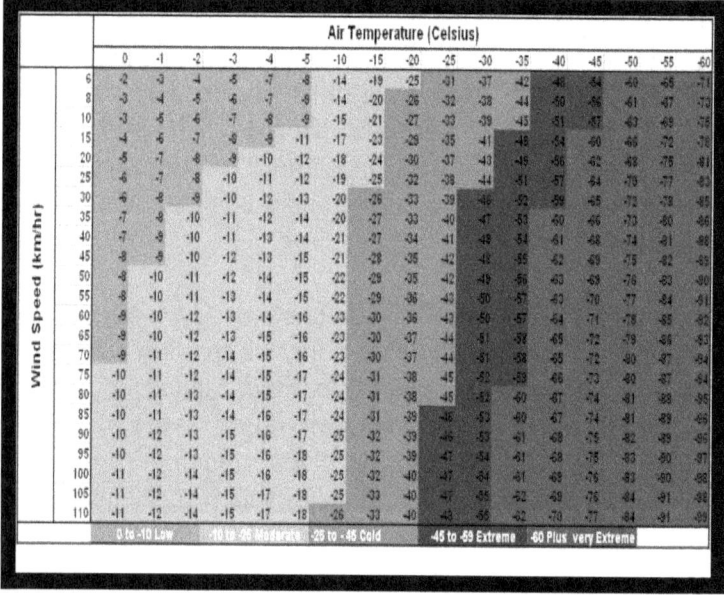

Wind Speed (km/hr)	Air Temperature (Celsius)																
	0	-1	-2	-3	-4	-5	-10	-15	-20	-25	-30	-35	-40	-45	-50	-55	-60
6	-2	-3	-4	-5	-7	-8	-14	-19	-25	-31	-37	-42	-48	-54	-60	-66	-71
8	-3	-4	-5	-6	-7	-9	-14	-20	-26	-32	-38	-44	-50	-56	-61	-67	-73
10	-3	-5	-6	-7	-8	-9	-15	-21	-27	-33	-39	-45	-51	-57	-63	-69	-75
15	-4	-6	-7	-8	-9	-11	-17	-23	-29	-35	-41	-48	-54	-60	-66	-72	-78
20	-5	-7	-8	-9	-10	-12	-18	-24	-30	-37	-43	-49	-56	-62	-68	-75	-81
25	-6	-7	-8	-10	-11	-12	-19	-25	-32	-38	-44	-51	-57	-64	-70	-77	-83
30	-6	-8	-9	-10	-12	-13	-20	-26	-33	-39	-46	-52	-59	-65	-72	-78	-85
35	-7	-8	-10	-11	-12	-14	-20	-27	-33	-40	-47	-53	-60	-66	-73	-80	-86
40	-7	-9	-10	-11	-13	-14	-21	-27	-34	-41	-48	-54	-61	-68	-74	-81	-88
45	-8	-9	-10	-12	-13	-15	-21	-28	-35	-42	-48	-55	-62	-69	-75	-82	-89
50	-8	-10	-11	-12	-14	-15	-22	-29	-35	-42	-49	-56	-63	-69	-76	-83	-90
55	-8	-10	-11	-13	-14	-15	-22	-29	-36	-43	-50	-57	-63	-70	-77	-84	-91
60	-9	-10	-12	-13	-14	-16	-23	-30	-36	-43	-50	-57	-64	-71	-78	-85	-92
65	-9	-10	-12	-13	-15	-16	-23	-30	-37	-44	-51	-58	-65	-72	-79	-86	-93
70	-9	-11	-12	-14	-15	-16	-23	-30	-37	-44	-51	-58	-65	-72	-80	-87	-94
75	-10	-11	-12	-14	-15	-17	-24	-31	-38	-45	-52	-59	-66	-73	-80	-87	-94
80	-10	-11	-13	-14	-15	-17	-24	-31	-38	-45	-52	-60	-67	-74	-81	-88	-95
85	-10	-11	-13	-14	-16	-17	-24	-31	-39	-46	-53	-60	-67	-74	-81	-89	-96
90	-10	-12	-13	-15	-16	-17	-25	-32	-39	-46	-53	-61	-68	-75	-82	-89	-97
95	-10	-12	-13	-15	-16	-18	-25	-32	-39	-47	-54	-61	-68	-75	-83	-90	-97
100	-11	-12	-14	-15	-16	-18	-26	-32	-40	-47	-54	-61	-69	-76	-83	-90	-98
105	-11	-12	-14	-15	-17	-18	-25	-33	-40	-47	-55	-62	-69	-76	-84	-91	-98
110	-11	-12	-14	-15	-17	-18	-26	-33	-40	-48	-56	-62	-70	-77	-84	-91	-99

| 0 to -10 Low | -10 to -25 Moderate | -25 to -45 Cold | -45 to -59 Extreme | -60 Plus very Extreme |

Calculating Wind Chill

PREVENTION: Understanding the Heat Index

The heat index is how hot the temperature really is once humidity is added to the equation. Use the chart below to calculate:

	Temperature (F) versus Relative Humidity (%)					
°F	90%	80%	70%	60%	50%	40%
80	85	84	82	81	80	79
85	101	96	92	90	86	84
90	121	113	105	99	94	90
95		133	122	113	105	98
100			142	129	118	109
105				148	133	121
110						135

HI	Possible Heat Disorder:
80°F - 90°F	Fatigue possible with prolonged exposure and physical activity.
90°F - 105°F	Sunstroke, heat cramps and heat exhaustion possible.
105°F - 130°F	Sunstroke, heat cramps, and heat exhaustion likely, and heat stroke possible.
130°F or greater	Heat stroke highly likely with continued exposure.

Calculating Heat Index

Direct sunlight can add up to 15 degrees F to the heat index.

Seeking Good Shelter

An effective physical structure or barrier is the first part of the shelter equation. Keep the following general concepts in mind when you locate or build a shelter:

Sturdy: It should withstand the elements and human activity.

41

Safe: It should protect you from the elements, animals, and other humans.

Warm: It should internally heat through fire, sunlight, insulation, and/or a small size that takes advantage of body heat.

Dry: It shouldn't leak.

Convenient: It should be located close to your other priorities (water, fire, etc.)

Remember the smaller the area, the easier to heat. It's much easier to warm a single room or tent than it is to heat your whole house, for example, if you find yourself without heat in the winter. You can even build a small shelter out of furniture or mattresses.

Wearing Protective Clothing

Clothing is the other part of the equation. Keep a spare set of clothes around to change into if yours get wet or ruined.

Cold Weather Survival: Dress in layers, allowing air space between the clothing items to help warm you, to insulate you. The layer closest to your body, like synthetic long underwear, should wick away moisture. The middle layer, like a wool sweater or synthetic jacket, should breathe and stay dry. Your outer layer should provide water and wind protection.

Wear a hat to keep your head warm; you can lose 40 percent of body heat through the head alone. Take care to wear warm, water-resistant shoes or boots when called for.

Remember mittens allow fingers to help warm each other, so they're warmer than gloves. You can use balled up newspaper or cardboard for insulation in a pinch.

For cold weather clothing materials, avoid cotton, denim, and corduroy: They hold moisture and take a long time to dry. Instead, seek out wool, fleece, the synthetic Dacron, the synthetic Gore-Tex, and especially the synthetic polypropylene. Goosedown or synthetic down is warm, but it loses all insulation ability when wet.

Hot Weather Survival: Wear lightweight, light-colored, and loose-fitting clothing. Wear a hat and sunglasses to protect your head and eyes from the sun. You lose more sweat through a naked body part than through a clothed one, so resist the urge to strip off clothing. Remember to use sunscreen.

For hot weather clothing materials, seek out cotton, linens, and the synthetic polypropylene for breathability. Avoid denim, corduroy, wool, and fleece.

A clothing material that functions quite well for both cold and hot weather conditions is the synthetic polypropylene. You can easily find it in sporting goods, outdoors, and army/navy stores, if not elsewhere.

Using Basic Knots

You may need to know a few basic knots for building a shelter or other tasks like securing a bandage. Knots can get very complicated and exotic, but here some basic ones that will serve you well:

Overhand Knot (Thumb Knot): Use it to place a marker or thick spot on the rope or to prevent the end from unraveling. Use it when you want the knot to be more permanent:

Overhand Knot

Square Knot (Reef Knot): Use it to join two ropes together:

Square Knot

Clove Hitch: Use it to tie a rope to a post or other object. Use it when you want the knot to only be temporary:

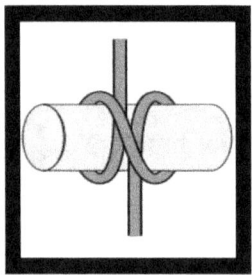

Clove Hitch

Double Half Hitch (Two Half Hitches): Use it to tie a rope to a post or other object or to tie a parcel. It's more secure than the clove hitch:

Double Half Hitch

Figure of Eight Knot: Use it to place a marker or thick spot on the rope or to prevent ropes from escaping. You can use it to replace the overhand knot:

Figure of Eight Knot

Bowline: Use it to make a fixed loop that won't tighten:

Bowline

Sheepshank: Use it to shorten, remove slack from, or bypass a frayed portion of a rope that you don't want to cut:

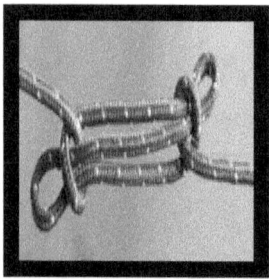

Sheepshank

Priority Three: Water

At a minimum for the short term, you need a gallon of water per day to survive, which doesn't leave very much for hygiene and cooking. That water has to come from stored or found sources, and it must be purified.

PREVENTION: Practicing Water Safety

You need to know how to be safe around a body of water, whether it's a backyard pool or lake. Most importantly, learn to swim: The American Red Cross and other organizations offer swimming classes for people of any age. Never swim alone; always have a buddy. Always obey the rules and lifeguard instructions, and swim only in lifeguard-supervised areas. Don't swim if you are tired, cold, or far from safety; also, be aware of your water environment and its hazards, such as strong currents and deep and shallow areas. Pay attention to weather forecasts and avoid swimming in bad weather. Only dive head-first into water when the area is marked for it; otherwise, always enter feet first. Don't mix alcohol with swimming. Finally, take extra precautions with children or new swimmers, like wearing flotation devices.

If you have a backyard pool or spa, keep the following additional cautions in mind:

Training: Learn basic first aid, including how to respond to water emergencies.

Children: Never leave children unattended when they are in or near the pool. Train them to not go near the pool without you (do the same with your pets). Enclose the pool completely with a locked fence (minimum 4-feet high).

Don't leave furniture near the fence that would make it climbable. Consider using an alarm system as well.

Postings: Post your pool rules--like no running--and enforce them consistently. Also post CPR and first aid instructions. In addition, post depth markers and, when appropriate, "no diving" signs.

Maintenance: Completely remove pool covers when the pool is in use, and make sure they are fastened securely when it's not in use. Keep all suction outlets (drains) covered. Keep the pool water clean, regularly tested, and chemically treated.

Storage: Store clearly labeled pool chemicals in secure, childproof containers. Store basic lifesaving equipment near the pool and learn how to use it. Equipment can include a small first-aid kit, flotation devices like life jackets, rope, and a pole. Keep a phone nearby when the pool is in use.

Follow similar cautions if you own a hot tub or spa. Remember it only takes a small amount of water to cause a drowning.

Storing Water

Make sure you have enough water stored to get your family and pets through two weeks minimum, and store it in a cool place out of direct sunlight. Keep the water in clear, hardy, plastic containers that won't break down over time (like 2-liter pop bottles, but never empty milk containers). Switch out the water every six months: Label it by date to help in keeping track. Also keep some empty containers, even large 50-gallon drums, on hand to fill in an emergency. If you store tap water, add four drops of bleach per gallon (two drops for a 2-liter bottle).

It's not the best idea to fill your bathtub during an emergency because the water evaporates and collects microorganisms so quickly. Also, never eat if you don't have water, no matter how hungry you feel.

Finding Water

Where else can you get water if your stores run out and your taps aren't working? You can't absolutely count on disaster agencies for help, so you need to know how to find and collect water from ground water, wells, rain, snow, morning dew, transpiration, solar stills, and even your own home. Scrounging and bartering for water are possible options, too.

Ground Water: This includes water you find from lakes, ponds, rivers, and even sidewalk puddles. Moving water from streams and rivers is usually much cleaner than stagnant water. Never collect water from sewers, and never drink saltwater from the ocean. Ever. Always purify water collected this way.

Wells: Wells aren't as common in the city as in the country, but they do provide a great source of water if you can find one. It takes a tremendous amount of energy to dig your own well, however. Purify water from an untested well.

Rain: Rain is of course unpredictable, but it's one of your best options for relatively clean water. The trick is to use a large surface area, like a sloped roof, to collect it. The water will collect in the gutters, and you just have to make sure that the downspout drops into a large barrel or other container. Make sure the roof and gutters are kept as clean and free of debris as possible. You can also use large tarps that drain in a V shape into containers as another way to collect rainwater. Even an inflatable swimming pool would work in a pinch if you have one. Always purify water collected this way.

Snow: Only collect snow that is far away from human and animal contamination, and never eat it, which causes you to lose too much body heat. Instead, melt it in a container over a fire. You will only get about one portion of water for every ten portions of snow, so you will need to melt a lot of it. Make sure you have plenty of fuel for all that melting. Always purify water collected this way.

Morning Dew: You can collect morning dew at dawn by running a clean cloth over damp grass and non-poisonous flowers, then wringing out the cloth every so often into a bowl. It's quite a bit of work for a small amount of water, but it is an option if you're really desperate. Always purify water collected this way.

Transpiration: You can collect water from non-poisonous tree or shrub leaves using a transparent bag. Place the bag over the branch and seal it tightly. Water will condense and fill at the bag's bottom, and you can drain it out into a bucket by cutting a small hole in the bag. Don't do this too long to a branch in hot weather because the branch will eventually die. No purification is needed.

Solar Stills: This excellent method gets you water that's already purified, so make sure you always have a metal shovel, clear plastic sheet, and clean container to collect water on hand. Simply dig a conical hole that comes to a point at the bottom (about 2 feet deep and 4 feet wide).

Place the container at the bottom middle point, cover the hole with the clear plastic sheet, put weights of some sort, like stones, around the sheet to anchor it, and finish by placing another weight in the middle of the sheet directly over the container. As ground water evaporates, it condenses against the underside of the sheet and drips into the container.

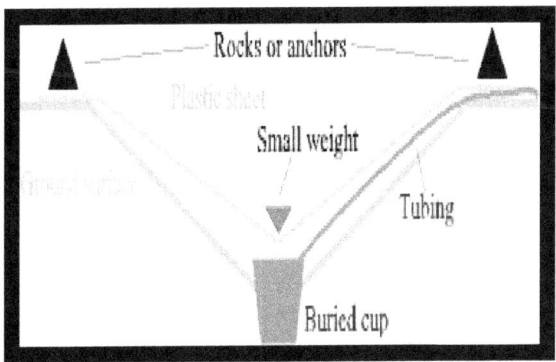

Solar Still

You'll get a better yield if you dig in a sunny spot. If possible, dig in areas with lots of greenery as well. Move to a new spot after 2 or 3 days. Optionally, you can access the purified water without removing the plastic sheeting by using plastic tubing.

Water Pipes: Even if your home's water pressure is off, there will be some leftover water in your pipes: To access it, open the highest cold water faucet (to let in air) and then open the lowest cold water faucet (to drain). Make sure you have a container to collect the water. This won't work for your hot water pipes. No purification is needed if collected right away.

Hot Water Heater: You can also gather up to 40 gallons of clean water from your home's hot water heater. Turn off the power or gas to your water heater first; if you forget, you may start a fire. With a container ready, open the faucet at the bottom of the water heater to access the water stored inside. Be aware that some hot water heaters don't have a faucet at their base. Check ahead of time because you can always have a plumber install one for you. No purification is needed if collected right away.

Freezer: You can also get water from your freezer. Never use water from your toilet tank or waterbed, however. No purification is needed if collected right away.

Scrounging or Bartering: In an emergency, the universe and its cousins will probably descend upon and clean out grocery stores, "big box" stores, and so on. If you are willing to risk the dangers of panicked humans, you may get lucky and be able to buy, barter for, or scrounge water this way. Early bird catches the worm.

Purifying Water

These sources generally provide you with clean water: bottled water, stored tap water that has had bleach added to it, your home's water pipes, your hot water heater, your freezer, tested wells, and solar stills. Water gathered from all other sources must be purified (and even these sources listed are only safe for a limited time). One of the most important skills for survival is how to purify water so that you don't get sick from it.

There are other methods, but those listed below are the simplest:

Straining/Filtering: This is a good first step because it gets rid of larger contaminants in the water; the water still won't be safe to drink, though. Strain the water through a coffee filter, paper towel, typing paper, or clean cotton cloth.

Boiling: After you've strained the water, you can bring it to a boil to make it safe to drink. No more purification occurs after 10 minutes of boiling.

Adding Bleach: Instead of boiling, you can add bleach to make the water safe to drink. Make sure you use basic, unscented bleach. Use a medicine dropper to add 2 drops of bleach for each 2-liter container (double to 4 if the water is very cloudy) or 4 drops for each gallon container (double to 8 if the water is very cloudy). If it doesn't smell like chlorine, you need to add more bleach. Mix together and let sit overnight or for at least one hour (the longer it sits, the purer it gets). You can add a crushed vitamin C tablet to neutralize the chlorine taste. Bleach loses its effectiveness over time, so make sure your household bleach is not over a year old.

Using Solar Disinfection: This method uses the sun's rays to make the water safe to drink and only works well in sunny, hot weather. Shake and place a clear container of water sideways in direct sunlight for at least six hours, using a shallow depth of water. You can use reflectors, like aluminum foil, to concentrate the sunlight. If the water reaches a temperature of 122 degrees Fahrenheit for at least one hour, it is then safe to drink.

Using Water Purification Tablets: These can be found online, in outdoors stores, or in army/navy outlets. They have a shelf life of about four years and should be protected from any moisture. Make sure you read the directions carefully so that you know how many tablets to dissolve into your 2-liter or gallon water containers and how long to wait before drinking the water. Water purification tablets don't kill certain parasites or chemicals that can make you sick, but they do work for most water.

Using a Water Purifier: An excellent method to purify water once it's been strained is to use a commercial water purifier. They are expensive but can often be found even in "big box" stores. Some are sized for water bottles, others for large containers of water. Make sure you read the directions carefully and replace cartridges as required.

You can make water taste better in general by shaking it vigorously to aerate it.

Priority Four: Fire

Fire can become more of a priority than water when cold weather threatens survival. It warms us, enables us to cook, gives us light, and cheers our spirits.

PREVENTION: Practicing Fire Safety

Open Fires: Always start a campfire in a contained area, like a fire pit, and clear the ground of debris five feet around it. Be especially careful of tree branches above. Store your fuel upwind and well away from the fire, and keep a bucket of water and a shovel nearby to put out the fire in an emergency. Never leave a fire, even a candle, unsupervised.

Appliances: Clean out toasters and dryer lint traps regularly.

Alarms and Extinguishers: Install and maintain smoke alarms on every floor of your home, especially near the bedrooms. Test them monthly and change the batteries twice a year. Place a fire extinguisher on every floor as well, especially near the kitchen and garage. Make them easily accessible, test them monthly, and practice how to use them.

Safety Plan: Have a fire escape plan: a place to meet up if there's a fire and two ways out of every room. Practice the plan to make sure everyone knows it. Make sure your address is clearly visible from the street to help firefighters locate your home in an emergency. Teach children about fire safety and store matches and lighters out of their reach.

Emergency Actions: If you catch on fire, stop, drop to the ground, and roll around to try to smother the flames. If you are in a fire, keep low to the floor where there's cleaner air, cover your mouth with a damp cloth if possible, get to the nearest safe exit, and never go back inside for anything. If a door is hot (feel with the back of your hand) or if there's smoke under it, don't open it. If you can't escape, try to reach a window and signal for help. Only try to fight a fire in its early stages, and never let a fire block your exit.

PREVENTION: Practicing Electrical Safety

Appliances: Turn off and unplug appliances if they smell or smoke. Don't use them if they have faulty wiring. Don't leave appliances where they can come into contact with water.

Cords: Don't use faulty cords. Don't place them underneath rugs or furniture or staple or nail them to walls or other objects. Don't place them in high traffic areas. Only use extension cords temporarily, never permanently. Only use good quality, certified surge protectors.

Outlets: Don't overload outlets. Replace any missing or broken wall plates. Replace outlets that have loose-fitting plugs. Place safety covers over any unused outlets that children can reach. Never try to force a plug into an outlet if it doesn't fit.

Lighting: Use the correct wattage light bulbs for their light fixtures and make sure the bulb is screwed in securely. Keep halogen floor lamps well away from any combustible material and turn them off if you leave the room for a long time.

Fuses and Circuit Breakers: Replace fuses and circuit breakers with the correct size.

Outdoors: Never mow the lawn if it's raining or the grass is wet. Stay at least 10 feet away from all power lines.

Space Heaters: Keep space heaters at least 3 feet away from any combustible materials, turn them off and unplug them when not in use, and never use them with an extension cord.

Maintenance: Have a licensed electrician make home electrical repairs and installations.

Starting a Fire

You can easily start a fire with lighters and matches, but what other tools are available? Flint kits are cheap, easy to use, and provide a good backup to your backup (applying the Rule of Threes). As for your matches, remember that they absorb moisture over time (even the waterproof ones) and should be enclosed in an airtight container, like a film canister. Remember that fires are much easier to start if you have firestarter (full log or pocket size).

A magnifying glass can start a fire on a hot day. Just focus the sun through the lens to a small point on some tinder. When the tinder starts to smoke, gently blow on it until it bursts into flame.

You can also use a small battery and wire to start a fire. Peel back the insulation off the wire, insulate your hands with gloves to avoid burning yourself, hold the exposed wire ends to both ends of the battery, wait for the wire to heat up, place the glowing wire against your tinder, and gently blow until it catches fire.

If you don't have a small wire, you can use a small strip of steel wool instead. Insulate your hands with gloves, hold one end of the steel wool against the bottom of the battery, rub the other end against the battery's top, wait for it to spark, place it against your tinder, and gently blow until it catches fire.

Fueling a Fire

Fires need a constant supply of air, so be sure to provide a way for the air to get to the burning fuel. Don't pack your fuel too tight, in other words. Fires also burn upward, and the hottest part is the tip of the flame. Put whatever you want to burn right above the flame, in other words, not below or beside it. They also need to begin small and build up to the firewood. Don't try to burn a big log in a small flame, in other words.

The process of fueling usually begins with tinder, easily combustible items like cotton balls or paper. Next up is kindling (size of a pencil). After that comes squaw wood (size of a child's arm). The process ends with true firewood, anything larger.

Teepee Fire: Often you'll want to start with a teepee fire because it's easy and utilitarian. Place your tinder at the base of a teepee-shaped structure that has kindling next, squaw wood outside of that, and firewood outside of that. This structure burns hot, protects the fire, and aims the smoke upward:

Teepee Fire

Log Cabin Fire: A log cabin fire is great modification to the teepee fire for quickly getting coals for cooking. Build a stacked square of logs around the fire with gaps between them to let in enough air. Lay it so that the top of the flames will catch and burn the top logs:

Log Cabin Fire

Hunter's Fire: Another good cooking fire is a hunter's fire: Place the top logs close together so that you can put a pot or pan on them:

Hunter's Fire

Star Fire: If you need to conserve fuel, make a star fire. Place three logs radiating out from the center, with the ends of the logs barely touching the flames. As the ends burn, slowly push in the logs:

Star Fire

Try to conserve fuel as much as possible. Remember that furniture, fences, and so on can provide fuel in an emergency. Try to burn clean fuel because carbon monoxide or other noxious fumes can make you sick or even kill you: Always give yourself enough ventilation.

Providing Alternate Light and Heat

Fire of course is not your only method for lighting when you don't have electricity. Battery-powered lanterns and LED flashlights work well, but be sure to stock up on batteries and spare bulbs. You can also use kerosene or propane lanterns; again, make sure you have plenty of kerosene and/or propane. Solar-powered and/or hand-crank lamps are a good possibility, if not a little harder to find. Light sticks work for short-term lighting: They only last for a few hours but are cheap and don't get hot.

You have other methods than fire for heat as well when the power's out. A portable catalytic heater is an excellent option. Battery-powered space heaters work well but require plenty of batteries. Propane or kerosene camp stoves are another option: Make sure you have extra propane and/or kerosene, though. Chemical hand or foot warmers are cheap and work for hours. Another simple trick for heat involves heating rocks in a fire, carefully placing the rocks in a fireproof bucket, and then letting the hot rocks warm a small space. This method can work for hours. Avoid wet rocks, though, like those found in stream beds.

Priority Five: Food

Although you can last a few weeks without food, you're miserable and don't function very well without it.

PREVENTION: Practicing Food Safety

Washing: Wash your hands often, including before preparing food and after handling raw meats, poultry, or seafood. Wash your utensils, plates, cutting boards, and thermometers between uses. Wash your dishcloths and towels often, using the hot cycle. Keep your appliances and countertops washed clean.

Disinfecting: Disinfect your sponges often, using a chlorine bleach solution. Replace them frequently.

Cooking: Cook your foods to safe temperatures. Use a meat thermometer for meats, poultry, seafood, and egg dishes.

Storing: Store raw meats, poultry, and seafood on the bottom shelf of the refrigerator so that they don't drip onto other foods. Keep the raw meats and other foods separate from each other. Place washed produce in clean containers, not the original containers you bought it in.

Refrigerating: Refrigerate foods quickly, within one hour of the meal. Make sure the refrigerator is set below 40 degrees Fahrenheit, and keep a refrigerator thermometer inside. Throw out leftovers in a timely manner. Cooked seafood and meat, in particular, are only good for one or two days.

Other: Use plastic, not wooden, cutting boards. Use clean scissors or knives to open bags of food. Use separate utensils for stirring and tasting food. Wear gloves if you have an open wound or sore on your hand.

Here are the generally accepted minimum safe cooking temperatures (in Fahrenheit) for these common foods:

Fresh Beef, Veal, or Lamb: 145 degrees (Medium Rare)
Ground Beef: 160 degrees
Chicken, Turkey, Rabbit, Duck, or Goose: 180 degrees
Fresh Pork, Ham, or Sausage: 160 degrees (Medium)
Deer: 165 degrees
Casseroles or Sauces: 160 degrees

Storing Food

Keep a 2-week minimum supply of food in your home in a cool, dry place, like a pantry, basement, or interior room. Always keep food sealed tightly and off the floor so that it doesn't rust or mold. Make sure it's protected from rodents and bugs. Most foods expire and/or lose their nutrients over time, so make sure you rotate your supply and keep track. Some items need to be replaced every six months, some every year, and some every two years, but that's a lot to organize: Just rotate every six months to keep your system conservative and simple. Sugar and salt can keep indefinitely if they are stored in metal or glass containers.

Finding Food

How do you acquire food in the city if your own stores run out? Here are some short-term possibilities:

Emergency food banks: Stay informed to see if disaster agencies have any set up.

Grocery and "big box" stores: Stay informed to see if any are open.

Neighbors: Consider trading or bartering with them.

City or private gardens: Use them for fruits and vegetables.

Local waters: Use them for fish, but be wary of high mercury levels.

City parks and streets: Use them for rabbits, squirrels, and other game.

Long-term food sources in a city would be difficult, but not impossible, but a two-week basic timespan, long enough to get you through most emergencies, shouldn't be too hard. Remember, most humans can survive three weeks without food if they have to.

Cooking Food

If you have electricity, cooking isn't an issue. But how do you cook if you don't have power? Your stored foods should include foods that don't need cooking, of course, but it's still good to have other options:

Flameless food heaters: These are specifically designed for MREs and backpacker meals.

Camp stove: Use outdoors, never indoors.

Charcoal or gas grill: Use outdoors, never indoors.

Wood stove: Make sure it vents to the outside.

Fireplace or campfire

Sterno

Car engine: Prepare the food, wrap it in aluminum foil, find a snug spot on your engine for the food, drive, and keep in mind that it will cook slower than in a conventional oven.

Solar oven: You use sunlight as your fuel, so this only works outdoors on a sunny day. Use a dark, thin, shallow metal pot to absorb the most heat, and use shiny surfaces around the pot to reflect extra sunlight onto it. There are many possible solar oven designs, but many of them rely on the same principle as the Greenhouse Effect to work, trapping heat inside the oven. Let in sunlight above the pot, but then trap it inside the oven with a transparent barrier (clear plastic bag, clear plastic cover, inverted glass bowl, etc.)

Priority Six: Hope

What are ways to keep your hopes and spirits up during an emergency? This may sound like a frivolous concern, but it's not: Remember that most humans won't last a long time without hope.

Keeping Your Hopes Up

If you have to evacuate, the items you bring with you should of course be small and limited, so think hard about what you need and apply the Rule of Threes. If you are staying put or sheltering in place in your home, plan around that as well. Here are some common methods people use to stay positive (you may very well have your own):

Family: Even if you can't be with your family during an emergency, you can have some favorite pictures of them or a small token that reminds you of them or of a favorite memory.

Close Friends: Again, your friends may not be with you during an emergency, but you can have some pictures of them or a small token that reminds you of them.

Religion and/or Spiritual Path: Having a small item or book, something that ties you to your religion or spiritual path, can do wonders.

Pets: For many, their pets are like their family, and simply having the animals there (or maybe just pictures of the animals) can make them feel a lot better.

Games: Having something fun to do to pass the time is a great idea. You can use a deck of cards, a portable gaming system, a small chess set, or whatever you like. Remember extra batteries as needed.

Music: The right music can lift the spirits of just about anyone. You may not be able to haul a computer, laptop, or stereo, but what about a small MP3 player? Remember extra batteries as needed.

Hobbies: Can you bring or have something that represents your favorite hobby? If you enjoy writing, for example, maybe you can make sure you have pen and paper. Or a good book if you like to read. Maybe even some knitting supplies if you like to knit or a camera if you take photographs.

Comfort Items: These include any items that make your day a little bit easier. Some people love coffee, for example. Others love chocolate.

Part 4: Other Priorities

This part addresses your other concerns and priorities in a survival situation. They don't always apply to the situation, but when they do, they are often just as important as the basic priorities covered in **Part 3**.

- First Aid
- Hygiene and Waste Disposal
- Communication
- Defense
- Finance
- Navigation
- Transportation
- Pets

First Aid

PREVENTION: Practicing Poison Safety

Emergency Number: Write down and program into your phones the number for the Poison Control Center: 800-222-1222.

Medicines: Keep pills in their original containers. Never keep medicines beside your bed or on counters. Follow medicine directions carefully to avoid overdoses. Check expiration dates regularly and discard as needed.

Children: Keep all medicines, vitamins, and household cleaning items out of the reach of babies and children. Poison-proof any areas where babies and infants have access. Keep poisonous plants out of the reach of babies and children. Securely close containers that use cake deodorizers.

Generators: Don't use a portable generator inside an enclosed building.

PREVENTION: Practicing Home Safety

Emergency Numbers: Write down and program into your phones your local police department, fire department, and the Poison Control Center.

Stairways and Hallways: Keep all stairways and hallways well-lit and clear of any clutter. Equip all stairways with handrails.

Kitchens: Clean up spills and wet spots right away. Turn off your oven and other appliances when you're not using them. Turn pot handles toward the back of the stove.

Bathrooms: Have night lights between bedrooms and bathrooms. Have a rubber mat and support bar in every bathtub or shower stall. Make sure hair dryers and other appliances are kept away from water and unplugged when not in use.

Outdoors: Keep outdoor walkways clear of ice.

Other: Keep all sharp objects and tools out of reach of children. Attach rugs to the floor with double-sided tape. Have a sturdy step stool to reach high cabinets. Check and maintain heating and cooling systems annually. Follow the steps under **Practicing Carbon Monoxide Safety, Practicing Water Safety**, **Practicing Fire Safety**, **Practicing Electrical Safety**, **Practicing Food Safety**, and **Practicing Poison Safety.**

PREVENTION: Getting Immunizations

Always make sure you and your family stay current on important immunizations. The CDC (Centers for Disease Control) recommends the following schedule:

Diptheria, Tetanus, Pertussis (DTaP): at 2 months, 4 months, 6 months, 15-18 months, 4-6 years, 11-12 years, and then diphtheria and tetanus boosters (Td) every 10 years after

Inactivated Polio (IPV): at 2 months, 4 months, 6-18 months, and 4-6 years

Measles, Mumps, Rubella (MMR): at 12-15 months and 4-6 years

H. Influenzae Type B (Hib): at 2 months, 4 months, 6 months, and 12-15 months

Hepatitis B (Hep B-1, B-2, and B-3): series starting at birth

Hepatitis A (Hep A): at 12-24 months

Pneumococcal Conjugate (PCV): at 2 months, 4 months, 6 months, 12-15 months, and 2 years

Varicella (Var): at 12-18 months and 4-6 years

Rotavirus (Rota): at 2 months, 4 months, and 6 months

Meningococcal (MCV4): at 2-10 years

Influenza: yearly as advised by your doctor

Pneumococcal: once at 65 years unless advised otherwise by your doctor

Follow your doctor's advice on immunizations, using this list as a general guideline. Children and teens should catch up on missed vaccines. Find out if you need certain other vaccines before traveling to other countries.

Moving an Injured Person

Never move an injured person unless they are in immediate danger, you have to get to someone else who needs immediate help, or you need to do so to provide the right care. Otherwise, don't do it because it often harms the person further. Here are ways to move an injured person if you must:

Blanket Drag: Roll the person into a blanket, gather the blanket at the person's head, and drag them to safety.

Clothes Drag: Gather the clothing at the person's neck and drag them to safety as you cradle their head with the clothes and your hands.

Foot Drag: Grasp the person's ankles and move backward in a straight line, dragging them with you to safety. Try not to bump the person's head.

Pack-Strap Carry: Position yourself with your back to the person, cross the person's arms in front of you, grasp their wrists, lean forward, pull the person onto your back, and carry them to safety.

Two-Person Seat Carry: Put an arm under the person's thighs and your other behind the person's back, interlock your arms with the other helper's arms, lift the injured person in the seat formed by your interlocking arms, and move the person to safety.

Walking Assist: Put the person's arm across your shoulders, hold it in place with one hand, place your other arm around the person's waist (possibly grabbing their belt or trouser top for leverage), and move the person to safety.

Placing Someone in the Recovery Position

If you are alone and need to leave the person for a moment to call 911 or to get a needed item, you should put them in what's called the Recovery Position, a body posture that helps to keep their airways open. Here's how you move someone into this position:

- Kneel at the person's side so that you can support their head and hip

- Take the arm further away from you and move it up next to their head

- Take the closer arm and cross it over their chest

- Bend the leg that's closer to you

- Gently roll the person away from you as you support their head and hip

- Make sure their head then angles toward the ground, which will allow any fluid to drain without choking them

- If the person starts to lose circulation or has been in the Recovery Position for longer than 30 minutes, turn them to the opposite side

Recovery Position

Recognizing a Fever

The easiest way to detect a fever is with an oral thermometer, recommended for adults and children older than 4 years. For newborns through 3 years old, use a rectal thermometer. You can also take an axillary (under the arm) reading for babies, but it's less accurate. Tympanic (ear) thermometers work well for older babies and children, but you have to be sure they are placed correctly and unhindered by ear wax. In general, digital thermometers are preferable. Avoid using mercury thermometers because of their health risks.

Always follow directions when using a thermometer, and be sure to sanitize it with rubbing alcohol between uses. Invest in disposable thermometer covers for extra protection. For the most accurate reading, make sure you wait at least 15 minutes after drinking or eating anything hot or cold.

For oral thermometers, anything over 99.5 degrees Fahrenheit is a fever.

For rectal or tympanic thermometers, anything over 100.4 degrees is a fever.

For axillary thermometers, anything over 99.0 degrees is a fever.

Typical body temperature varies somewhat person to person, and can even fluctuate throughout the day. Also, if you don't have a thermometer, you have a decent (though far from perfect) chance of detecting fever if you feel the person's forehead for hotness.

Recognizing an Infected Wound or Burn

Infection can start within days or even hours of an injury and should be taken seriously. Always wash your hands before and after treating a wound or burn, even if you wear disposable gloves. Wash minor wounds with soap and water and treat with antibiotic ointment. Follow your doctor's advice for major wounds, and change the bandages daily.

Look for the following signs of infection: redness, swelling, pus discharge, red streaks, fever and/or other illness.

Get medical attention if you suspect an infection.

Performing the Heimlich Maneuver

This maneuver may save a person's life if they are choking and can't breathe. If they can't cough, breathe, or speak (possibly clutching their throat as well), assume that they are choking and begin this maneuver.

On a Conscious Adult: If they are an adult, get them to stand, stand behind them, deliver five back blows with the heel of your hand between their shoulder blades, make a fist and place the thumb side against their upper abdomen (above the navel but below the ribcage), grasp your fist with your other hand, and press into their upper abdomen for five quick, upward thrusts. Repeat the process until you hopefully dislodge whatever is blocking their airflow. The same steps work for someone in a wheelchair.

Heimlich Maneuver

On a Pregnant or Large Adult: If they are pregnant or too big for you to reach around, change to chest thrusts instead of abdominal thrusts.

On an Infant: If an infant is choking, support them on your thigh with their head lower than their chest. You can do this while you stand or sit. Then gently give them five back blows with the heel of your hand and then five abdominal thrusts with your middle and index fingers. Repeat until you hopefully dislodge whatever is blocking their airflow.

On an Unconscious Adult: If they are unconscious, place them on their back and kneel astride their hips. Clear their airway with a finger sweep. With one hand on top of the other, place the heel of your bottom hand on their abdomen (above the navel but below the ribcage). Use your body weight to press into their abdomen for five quick, upward thrusts. Repeat until you hopefully dislodge whatever is blocking their airflow. Then begin CPR as needed.

On Self if Alone: If you are choking and you're alone, lean over, pressing your abdomen against any firm object, like a table, or give yourself five quick, upward abdominal thrusts.

If someone's airway is open enough that they can cough, speak, or cry, do not perform the Heimlich Maneuver.

Hygiene and Waste Disposal

PREVENTION: Washing Hands and Using Barriers

In a public restroom, unroll your paper towel ahead of time to avoid later contamination from the towel dispenser. Wet your hands in warm water, apply the soap to your hands, rub your hands together vigorously for at least 20 seconds (don't forget to scrub your nails), rinse your hands, dry them, and then turn off the faucet with the paper towel. Use the paper towel on the door handle as well.

To make sure you wash for 20 seconds, sing the ABC song in your head. Be aware that hand sanitizers, like Purell, clean your hands, but they don't take the place of using soap and water. Wash your hands at least every tenth time, if not more often. Also be aware that soap coming from open, refillable dispensers can become contaminated with microorganisms.

Don't cough or sneeze into your hands or into the air: Cover your nose and mouth with a tissue or your arm/sleeve. Avoid touching your face until you've washed your hands.

Protect yourself from infectious diseases and viruses through protective barriers. Infection can be passed through bodily fluids, bodily contact, and even the air. Always use disposable gloves when giving first aid to someone, and always use a CPR mask/breathing mask when performing resuscitation. Some situations may call for protective eyewear as well.

Be careful when you remove disposable gloves:

- Remove the first glove partway by pinching it at the wrist and pulling it toward the fingertips without totally taking it off. It should be half inside out

- Use the first glove to remove the second glove by pinching the outside of the second glove and pulling it off completely

- Finish removing the first glove by using your free hand to touch the clean interior surface of it

- Throw away the gloves in an appropriate container and immediately wash your hands

Take off rings and watches before wearing gloves, and never put gloves on over an open wound or sore on your hand (bandage the wound first). Double glove if you know you will be touching something particularly infectious, wet, or nasty.

PREVENTION: Caring for Eyes, Teeth, Ears, Feet

Eyes: Make sure you get annual eye exams, especially if you wear glasses or contact lenses. Follow hygiene directions carefully for contact lenses. Wear safety goggles or glasses as needed when working around hazardous materials or flying debris or playing certain sports. For children, avoid toys with sharp edges or points, and don't allow BB guns. Pad or cushion sharp corners on furniture and fixtures. Never stare directly at the sun, especially during a solar eclipse. You may want to consider Lasik eye surgery if you wear glasses or contact lenses.

If you get a small foreign body in your eye, like an eyelash, flush your eye with saline solution or purified water (tap water can be used but may cause some irritation). If that doesn't work, then use a cotton swab or tip of a tissue to remove the item after pulling back the upper or lower eyelid. Do not scrape the swab or tissue across your cornea, the clear dome over the iris. Never rub your eyes to remove a foreign body. If you get a larger foreign body in your eye, seek emergency medical care.

Teeth: Remember to take care of your teeth, even during an emergency. Have enough water stored for sanitation so that you can at least brush your teeth when you wake up and when you go to sleep each day, among other things. Floss each day and remember to swish for a full 30 seconds when using mouthwash.

See your dentist every 6 months for a check-up and cleaning. Make an appointment as well if you have tooth pain or sensitivity, an injured tooth, a change in your bite, swollen or reddened gums, or jaw pain. Avoid candy and sugary soda, and think twice before getting a tongue piercing.

Ears: Wax is your ears' natural protection against bugs, dust, and germs and shouldn't be removed from inside the ear with a Q-tip or other tool. You also risk puncturing your eardrum or pushing the wax in further and blocking the ear if you do so. Clean the outside of your ears, but never put anything inside them.

Be sure to protect your ears from hearing loss and get tested regularly if your job or hobbies expose you to loud noises. Wear ear protection when around loud machinery, music, or guns.

Feet: You must keep your feet warm and dry. Make sure you wear adequate footwear for cold, wet weather, and make sure you change your socks when they get wet. If your feet are cold indoors, take off your shoes and just wear socks to increase warmth and circulation.

You can give your footwear extra insulation by using thick wool inserts or cutting out cardboard insoles and placing them inside your shoes. Newspaper works for insulation as well.

Washing Clothes Without a Washing Machine

As long as you have detergent or soap and plenty of water, you can wash clothing even when there's a power outage:

- First, check the clothing label for the water temperature that you should use (cold, warm, or hot)

- Check the clothing for stains and pretreat them with a stain stick or small amount of detergent gently scrubbed into the spot

- Fill a sink or basin with a small amount of detergent and water of the correct temperature based on the clothing's labels. This should form suds.

- Mix your clothes around in the sudsy water for 10 to 15 minutes, making sure you pay attention to each article

- Rinse and wring out the excess water from each item

- Hang your wet clothes to dry. You can use hangers, furniture, flat surfaces, and so on

- Drain the used water before you begin another load of laundry

Washing clothing this way obviously uses up a lot of water, so decide carefully before doing so.

Cleaning up Blood or Bodily Fluid Spills

Wear disposable gloves and clean up the spill immediately. Wipe it up with paper towels then cover the area with a mixture of 1 part bleach per 10 parts water. Let the mixture stand for at least 10 minutes before cleaning or mopping up. The bleach/water mixture is effective for up to 24 hours.

Getting Rid of Waste

If you lose water pressure and can't flush your toilet, remember this trick: Pouring one gallon of water directly into the toilet will flush it. The water you use for this doesn't have to be purified, it can be recycled, but you should do this at least once a day to cut down on odors and such. Keep the toilet lid down and use a disinfectant spray (like Lysol) to help with odors. The lidded bucket you have with your home supplies is another option, of course.

If you find yourself in a survival situation where you are away from a toilet, you have a few methods available to deal with solid waste. Keep in mind that feces are full of bacteria, viruses, and worms, and that exposed feces attract flies, which also spread disease. Solid waste must be kept away from your survival priorities: air, shelter, water, fire, and food. Therefore, locate it downwind and at least 20 feet away from your shelter and at least 165 feet away from your water and food sources. Choose a site that won't flood and have soap and wash water available.

You can dig a pit latrine to deal with waste. If you only have a few people making waste, you can simply bury it in a shallow hole in the ground. If you have a larger group with which to contend, you'll want to dig a larger hole that has a close-fitting cover made out of any materials at hand. This keeps out flies and cuts down on odors. Try to place shallow drainage ditches around the pit to help protect it from flooding. Dig a new latrine once you have less than 2 feet between the surface and pit contents. You can dump sawdust, wood chips, or soil over the waste to limit odors.

There are fancier latrines that you can build, including a ventilated improved pit (VIP) latrine, but a basic pit latrine will certainly get you through at least 2 weeks.

Communication

Accessing Emergency Telephone Numbers

You probably already know to call 911 in an emergency.
Some cities have enhanced 911 systems that automatically
display your name, address, and phone number to the
dispatcher when you call in so that they can contact you if
the call gets dropped. Other cities only have basic 911,
which means the dispatcher can't call you back if you get
disconnected. No matter what, give the dispatcher your
location and phone number right away. Never program
your cell phone to call 911 with one button because you
may cause accidental 911 calls.

Here are other essential numbers to know: your police
department, fire department, and the Poison Control Center
(800-222-1222). Write these numbers down and program
them into your phones.

If you carry a cell phone, make sure you program in at least
one ICE (In Case of Emergency) contact for emergency
personnel to look up and call in case you get in an accident.
Choose someone who lives in the same city, and try to list
at least three ICE contacts.

Signaling for Help

- Stand with both of your arms stretched high while
  facing oncoming vehicles

- Hang a red triangle on your door or window or
  nearby

- Wave a white handkerchief

- Make three fires (or flares) in a triangle

- Write SOS or use Morse Code to sound or flash the letters: three dots, three dashes, three dots. Pause, then repeat

- Use the International Mountain Distress Signal: six flashes or whistles in a minute, then pause for a minute, then repeat

Be sure to keep both a whistle and signaling mirror in your bug out bag and home. Flares are good to have, too (at least three, of course). White or red cloth can be easily modified for your signaling needs.

Staying Informed

A hand-crank or battery-powered radio is the best way to stay informed during an emergency if the power is out. Some radios even come with cell phone chargers, flashlights, and so on. You should monitor the following sources for emergency information: local television and radio stations, which may use the Emergency Broadcast System, and local news internet sites. Be wary of news spread by word of mouth.

The U.S. Department of Homeland Security has developed a national threat advisory system for terrorist attack that you should check periodically:

Red: Severe risk of terrorist attack

Orange: High risk of terrorist attack

Yellow: Elevated/significant risk of terrorist attack

Blue: Guarded/general risk of terrorist attack

Green: Low risk of terrorist attack

You can access threat advisory information at their website, www.dhs.gov.

Defense

PREVENTION: Protecting Your Home

You want to protect your home with multiple layers of security so that it isn't a quick and easy target, which will deter almost all burglars:

Lighting: Keep some lights on even when you're not home and consider investing in outdoor security lighting.

Security Systems: Consider investing in a good home security system that automatically alerts the police. Be aware, though, that they are responsible for many false alarms that tie up police time and that standard response time is much longer than the time it takes for a burglar to finish and leave. Make sure you display the fact that you have a security system if you choose to get one. Also, consider getting a dog that will bark when there's an intruder. Again, display the fact that you have a dog. Get a home security safe for your valuables and important documents.

Doors: Make sure all outer doors are thick and have deadbolts and wide-angle peepholes. These include your front door, backdoor, and the door between your home and garage. Get strong locks and security bars for any sliding glass doors.

Windows: Make sure your windows are strong, and avoid window-mounted air conditioners in ground-floor windows. Keep hedges near windows well trimmed to avoid convenient hiding places. Don't advertise valuables like stereos or computers through your windows.

Outdoors: Don't leave anything that can be carried off in your yard. Lock all outdoor sheds. Don't leave an extra key under the doormat or anywhere hidden outside.

Other: Don't label your key ring with your home address. When you are away on a trip, have the post office hold all mail or have a trusted friend collect it for you so that it's not obvious that you're gone. Also, keep some lights on or even install timers for your lights to make it look like you're home.

PREVENTION: Protecting Your Computer

Firewalls: Make sure you have firewall protection and that it is turned on. This protects your computer from hackers.

Virus Protection: Make sure you have Antivirus protection and that it is set to update automatically. This protects your computer from malicious programs.

Spyware Protection: Make sure you have Antispyware protection and that it is set to update automatically. This protects your computer from programs that spy on your online activities without your consent.

Operating Systems: Make sure your operating system is up to date and that it is set up to notify you when it needs to update files. This protects your computer by patching security holes.

Passwords: If you ever leave your computer or laptop alone when it's on, make sure it has password protection. Change your passwords often.

Other: Never open an email attachment from someone you don't know or forwarded email attachments from people you do know. Be wary of downloads. Turn off your computer regularly.

PREVENTION: Staying Safe in the City

Sometimes you are just in the wrong place at the wrong time and can't avoid trouble, but many times you can. Living in the city is less dangerous if you keep the following general tips in mind:

Being Followed: If you think you are being followed on foot, do not confront the person or head toward dark areas. Instead, head toward a populated area and call the police. Never go home if you are being followed. If you think that you are being followed by someone in a car, turn and walk in the opposite direction, yelling if possible.

Locking Up: Always lock your doors and windows, even if you are leaving for just a few minutes. Never unlock your door without first verifying who is there through the peephole or a window. Never enter your home or apartment if the door is open. Call the police from your cell phone or a nearby pay phone. If you live in an apartment building, never allow someone you don't know to enter the building or buzz in strangers.

Walking: Do not walk alone at night. Don't take short cuts through deserted areas like alleys. Be extra wary when people ask you for money or directions. Reply from a distance, not letting them get too close to you. Stay alert at all times. Avoid wearing headphones or talking on your cell phone while walking, especially at night or in unfamiliar areas. Walk confidently and try to make eye contact with the people around you. If you look like a victim, you will naturally draw predators. Don't get on an elevator alone with someone if they make you uncomfortable.

Protecting Your Valuables: Keep cash in deep, interior pockets, not in a rear pocket. Keep handbags securely closed and worn around the neck diagonally across your body. If you don't have a cell phone, carry phone cards or money for emergency phone calls. Never loan your cell phone to a stranger, and keep it hidden when not in use.

Driving: Drive with your doors locked and windows up, especially if an area makes you nervous. Always scan the backseat of your car before you get in.

Drinking: Never leave your drink unattended if you are in a bar or nightclub. Also, never accept a drink from someone if you can't see it being prepared. Never leave a bar or nightclub with a stranger, and never ride with someone who has been drinking. Always have enough emergency money for cab fare.

Defending Yourself: Consider carrying pepper spray or some other legal weapon: Make sure you have the training to use it, though. Take a self-defense class or learn a martial art.

Other: Trust your instincts: If someone makes you uncomfortable, head for a populated area. Always let someone know where you are going and when you plan to return.

It's better to yell "Fire" than "Help" if you're ever attacked because bystanders are more likely respond to a situation that may affect them directly.

PREVENTION: Practicing Gun Safety

Handling: Keep the gun unloaded until ready to use (unless it's stored in a gun safe or lockbox). In addition, handle each gun like it's always loaded. Keep the gun pointed in a safe direction. Lay your finger outside the trigger guard, along the side of the gun, until ready to shoot. Think first, shoot second: Be aware of both your target and the area beyond your target. Never shoot if you have been drinking or have taken medication that can impair your abilities.

Maintaining: Learn how to operate and maintain the gun before using it. Read the owner's manual. Clean the gun regularly and after each use. If you're not sure if the gun is safe to operate, have a gunsmith inspect it. Use only the correct ammunition for the gun.

Wearing Protection: Wear eye and ear protection when practicing.

Storing: Store guns safely: Pick what best works for you and your family, whether it's a lockbox, gun safe, or other option.

Make sure you follow all laws, which can vary by state and locality. Consider taking a gun safety course.

PREVENTION: Keeping a Low Profile

Other panicked people can be just as dangerous as the emergency situation itself, so keeping a low profile is in your best interest. If you aren't evacuating but staying put in your home during an emergency, it's better not to have to leave, which means making sure you have all your supplies ahead of time.

Work together with your neighbors during an emergency, but don't advertise what you have because the desperate or ill-prepared may be tempted to take it from you. Think hard about who you let into your shelter: Even if you need to trade or barter, consider doing so in a neutral place.

If looting or violence becomes a concern, you can use fake signs to put off others from your shelter. *Beware of Dog*, for example. Board up your doors and windows as well.

If you must evacuate, keeping a low profile is much more difficult. Make the contents of your bug out bag and/or car private and covered as much as possible, hide any valuable items, and carry a fake wallet (with only a tiny portion of your actual cash) to hand to thieves in case you're mugged. As for the rest of your real cash, spread it out inside deep interior pockets.

Handling Law Enforcement Encounters

What to Avoid: Don't make sudden movements. Keep your hands in plain view, including resting them on the steering wheel if you're pulled over. Never touch the officer or their equipment. Never physically resist an officer. Don't pass behind the officer.

What to Record: Always record the officer's name and badge number. If you find reason to fill out a Police Misconduct Report, do so as soon as possible so that you can remember important details.

What to Say: Only speak to an officer if you are reporting a crime. Otherwise, just give your name and address. If the officer asks you anything beside your name and address, you are being interrogated, and you can protect yourself by stating that you are going to remain silent and that you want a lawyer. Keep repeating that if they continue to try to get information from you. Remember that anything you say can be held against you, and the officer can lie to try to get incriminating information from you.

If the officer asks for permission to search your pockets, glove compartment, and so on, tell them you do not consent to a search. They do have the right to pat you down and check your bags for weapons, however.

If an officer is detaining you, they must have reasonable suspicion, only detain you for a short time, and not change your detention location. If you are detained, you are not free to leave.

If an officer is arresting you, they must have probable cause and are allowed to search your body and bags. The officer searching your body must be of the same gender.

If the officer asks for permission to enter your home and they don't have a search warrant, step outside and tell them you do not consent to a search. They are legally allowed to enter any room that you go into, so don't go back inside.

If the officer has a search warrant, read it carefully and still tell them you do not give consent to a search in case the warrant has flaws. Step aside when they enter, though, and do not touch them in any way.

Choosing Weapons

Never use a weapon of any sort illegally or without proper training; this applies to your own body as well. Care for and maintain the weapon on a regular basis, and be wary of display and low-quality items. Keep in mind the strengths and shortcomings of the following weapon types:

Own Body (Martial Arts):
Legal
Always available
Free
High concealment
Training recommended
Requires close combat

Chemical Weapons (Pepper Spray, Mace):
Check legality (legal in most states)
Limited availability
Cheap
High concealment
Training not required
Requires close combat and risky in strong winds

Electrical Weapons (Taser, Stun Gun, Stun Baton):
Check legality
Limited availability
Expensive
Medium concealment
Training not required
Requires close combat

Edged Weapons (Knife, Axe, Sword, Broken Bottle):
Check legality
Easy availability

Cheap
High concealment unless sword
Training recommended
Requires close combat (unless throwing knives)

Bludgeoning Weapons (Baseball Bat, Baton, Crowbar):
Legal
Easy availability
Cheap
Low concealment
Training not required
Requires close combat and swinging room

Projectile Weapons (Handgun, Shotgun, Rifle, Submachine Gun):
Check legality
Limited availability
Expensive
Varied concealment
Training required
Requires gun permit and loud

Explosive Weapons (Molotov Cocktail, Grenade):
Illegal
Very limited availability (unless homemade)
Expensive (unless homemade)
Varied concealment
Training required
Very dangerous to make or use and loud

Choosing Body Armor

Remember that you have to be wearing the body armor for it to work, and a good rule of thumb is to have the type of body armor that will overprotect you from the guns you may reasonably face. The stronger the armor, the more difficult it is to wear. There are six formal classification types:

Type I: Protects you from .22 round nose and .380 round nose bullets.

Type II-A: Protects you from 9mm round nose and .40 bullets. Used full-time by many police forces.

Type II: Protects you from .357 Magnum soft point bullets. Heavier and bulkier than either Type I or II-A.

Type III-A: Protects you from high velocity 9mm round nose and .44 Magnum hollow point bullets. The highest level of protection available for concealable body armor.

Type III (Rifles): Protects you from 7.62mm (military M80) bullets. Intended for tactical situations where its use is warranted.

Type IV (Armor Piercing Rifles): Protects you from .30 armor piercing (military M2 AP) bullets. The highest level of protection currently available and intended for tactical situations where its use is warranted. Note that it is made of materials that may provide only single-shot protection.

Make certain that any purchased body armor is NIJ-certified. Avoid any vests made with Zylon, which has been decertified because of premature degradation. When buying armor, always check for heat buildup, freedom of movement, weight, concealment, comfort, and cost. Always make sure there is a money-back guarantee.

Protective helmets, riot shields, arm protectors, and other forms of protective wear are also available and can be found online.

Finance

PREVENTION: Protecting Your Identity

Identity theft is a growing problem in the United States and elsewhere, so make sure you protect yourself:

Documents: Completely shred any documents that contain personal information. Don't leave receipts at ATMs, gas stations, or sales counters. Don't leave your mail in your mailbox overnight. Don't carry your birth certificate or social security card: Keep them in a locked fireproof safe, or some other secure location.

Credit Reports: Review your credit reports with all three credit agencies every year. You are legally allowed a free copy of your credit report from each agency--Equifax, TransUnion, and Experian--once a year (in other words, a free report every four months). Just visit www.annualcreditreport.com and follow the directions.

Passwords: Change passwords often and don't write them down.

Account Numbers: Don't give your account numbers to telephone or mail solicitations or to a website unless it is a secure transaction.

Credit Cards: Contact your credit card issuer if you don't receive a replacement card prior to your old card's expiration date. Report lost or stolen credit cards immediately and sign new ones as soon as they arrive.

Financial Statements: Always check your monthly financial statements for errors.

Telemarketers: Consider registering with the National Do Not Call Registry, which blocks most telemarketing calls. Visit www.donotcall.gov for more information.

Fraud Alerts: Place a fraud alert on your credit file to tighten its security. An even stronger step would be to place a freeze on your credit file (only do this if you don't have plans to open any new credit accounts in the near future).

PREVENTION: Carrying Enough Insurance

Emergencies are bad enough without having to go broke over them. It's important to have enough insurance to protect yourself from economic collapse. Stay current with your insurance policy information and update whenever a change in circumstances warrants it. Also, keep records available with your other important documents to take with you if you have to evacuate.

You can often save money by "bundling" your insurance with one company that gives you a discount for having multiple policies with them. Sometimes the amount you save from bundling is more than the amount you pay for one of the policies!

Car Insurance: Car insurance is an absolute must if you own a vehicle, and it's actually illegal to not carry it in many states. Price around for the best offer because rates can vary significantly.

Homeowner's/Renter's Insurance: Carry either homeowner's or renter's insurance: the former if you own a home and the latter if you rent an apartment. Make sure you have a record, including a picture and ID number, for each major appliance or item you own, and keep this record in a fireproof safe or safety deposit box. If you have a backyard pool, make sure your homeowner's insurance covers it. Carry flood insurance if you live in an area prone to flooding. Be wary and learn what items are not covered.

Life/Disability Insurance: Make sure you have life insurance to protect your family in the event of your death. Disability insurance is recommended as well. Both of these often come with your job's benefits package, but check to make sure. If you don't get benefits, consider getting them on your own, especially if you have a family.

Medical Insurance: Many jobs also offer medical insurance, including dental and vision coverage, as part of their benefits package, but again check to make sure. Get it on your own if not: A leading cause of bankruptcy in the U.S. is high medical bills.

Other: Here are other forms of insurance that you should consider, based on your circumstances: motorcycle insurance, bicycle insurance, long-term care insurance, funeral insurance, and pet insurance. On the other hand, the following forms of insurance are often (but not always) a waste of money: mortgage insurance, flight insurance, and insurance on outstanding credit card balances. They are often already built in as part of your life or disability insurance and aren't competitively priced.

Using Cash and Trading

Keep hidden cash on hand. During an emergency, you may not be able to access banks or ATMs or use debit or credit cards. If evacuating or on the move, keep your "real" cash hidden, preferably in more than one spot, and a smaller amount in a fake wallet that you can hand to a mugger without losing your whole bankroll. Have plenty of ones and change, too.

What if you end up in a situation where you have to trade for what you need? It comes down to what you have to trade and your bargaining skills. No matter your skills (or lack thereof), you can at least prepare by having some of the items that will most likely gain value in an emergency. Think "portable" and "perishable"; in other words, these items tend to be small and quickly used up:

Matches and lighters
Batteries
Nails and screws
Unopened medicine (with expiration date)
Soap, toothpaste, other basic toiletries
Bottled water
Unopened food (with expiration date)
Coffee
Gas, kerosene, oil, propane, and other fuels
Firewood
Toilet paper
Cigarettes and alcohol
Ammunition

This list just gives you an idea: Every situation will breed a unique set of commodities.

When you trade with someone, make sure the other person really has what you want first. They may try to get you to invest time into the bargaining process so that you are more likely to take them up on their offer: Be ready for this common tactic.

Navigation

Navigating with Tools

Yes, a GPS (Global Positioning System) is tops for navigation. It's also expensive, around a few hundred dollars, though the price is dropping. Some cars, cell phones, or other items come with built-in GPS, or you can buy it as a handheld device. GPS is simple to use and can be accurate to within 3 meters if used correctly. As a navigation tool relying on technology, however, you should always have other methods at your disposal.

A compass is your next best method, one that is cheap and easy to use. You should own at least one compass no matter what.

Maps, of course, are always useful to have handy: Keep city, state, and country maps in your car and home. Remember that online maps won't necessarily be available during a power outage or if you have to evacuate quickly.

Navigating Without Tools

How do you tell direction if you are ever without GPS, compass, or map? If you are north of the Equator (Northern Hemisphere), you have other less precise methods:

Using Moss: Moss often grows on the northern side of tree trunks.

Using Clouds: Clouds often move from west to east, except in mountain regions.

Using the North Star: You can find north by locating the North Star, Polaris, in the night sky. First locate the Big Dipper constellation, then locate the two outer stars of the cup portion, then follow an imaginary line that continues from those two outer stars (about five times the distance) to locate Polaris.

Using a Watch and Shadow: Place a stick straight up into the ground so that it casts a shadow, and then place your watch next to it so that the hour hand is parallel to the stick's shadow. Find the halfway point between the hour hand and 12:00, and draw an imaginary line from that point through the center of the watch. You now have your north-south line (sun to the south). During the summer months of Daylight Savings Time, use 1:00 instead of 12:00.

Using Shadow: Place a stick straight up into the ground so that it casts a shadow. Mark the tip of the shadow it casts with another stick. Wait 10 minutes and mark the shadow tip again with another stick. Repeat again after another 10 minutes. After a total of 30 or 40 minutes, you'll have a row of sticks making an east/west line.

Understanding Interstate Patterns

Interstates and addresses in the United States follow a few general patterns (with exceptions, of course), and knowing them is useful:

- Primary interstates are always given one or two-digit numbers. East/west highways are given even numbers, and north/south highways are given odd numbers

- Even-numbered highways increase from west to east; odd-numbered highways increase from south to north

- Auxiliary highways off the main interstates are given three digits. They begin with an even number when they eventually loop back to the main interstate (called a loop) and begin with an odd number when they don't end at another interstate (called a spur). They are labeled east/west or north/south based on their general direction

- Even-numbered addresses are usually on the east or north side of the street; odd-numbered addresses are usually on the west or south

Transportation

PREVENTION: Protecting Your Car

Across the country, car thefts have skyrocketed. Any car can be stolen: The trick is to make sure yours isn't an easy mark. As far as basic preventative measures, always lock your doors and close windows when you leave your car, don't advertise a great sound system (use a detachable faceplate, for example), keep valuables out of sight, park in well-lighted areas or garages, and turn the wheels toward the curb when parallel parking on the street. Never leave a spare key or the car's title paperwork inside.

You should also invest in at least one active or passive anti-theft device. Active measures require you to remember to use them; passive measures are built-in and may lower your car insurance rate. Here are some of the most common devices:

Steering wheel lock, like the Club (active; visible)
Steering column lock (active; visible)
Tire/wheel lock (active; visible)
Brake pedal lock (active; visible)
VIN etching on windows and parts (passive; visible)
Audible car alarm (passive; hidden)
Decals that advertise a car alarm (passive; visible)
Kill switch (active; hidden)
Smart keys (passive; hidden)
Electronic tracking (passive; hidden)

Your best defense is to use a multi-layer defense of more than one anti-theft device.

PREVENTION: Practicing Driving Safety

Wearing a Seat Belt: Always wear a seat belt with a shoulder restraint when riding in front or back seats. Use car safety seats correctly for infants and children and never place them in the front passenger seat.

Avoiding Impairment: Don't drink and drive, and don't drive on medications that impair your driving ability. Don't drive if you are exhausted.

Avoiding Distractions: Don't talk on a cell phone while driving. Even using a hands-free kit distracts you, though not as much as using a hand-held phone. Don't eat, drink hot beverages, apply makeup, or try to read while driving. Don't drive with the music so loud that you can't hear approaching emergency vehicles. Don't overload your car with passengers, and secure any items from hitting you in the head if you have to brake suddenly. Adjust mirrors, seats, and accessories before you begin moving.

Driving Defensively: Try to think of errors the other drivers could make and be ready to react. Leave enough clearance when you drive by parked cars: This protects you from hitting them if their doors suddenly fly open. Don't tailgate other drivers. Allow at least a 4-second space between your cars. Always use turn signals when you make a turn or change lanes. If you are using a multiple lane road, use the left lane only when you are passing a vehicle. Remember that trucks make wide right turns and that they have many blind spots. If you can't see the driver, he or she can't see you. Always drive with your headlights on. Stay under the speed limit.

Driving in Inclement Weather: In snowy or rainy weather, don't hit your brakes suddenly, but slowly. Leave extra space for braking. Keep spare windshield washer fluid handy in case you suddenly run out. Don't drive without first clearing snow and ice from all windows, headlights, and taillights. If you have a rear-wheel drive vehicle, carry some extra weight in the back to help with traction. This can be sand or rock salt, for example, which can also be used to get unstuck from snow.

Other: Consider taking a defensive driving course. Never pick up hitchhikers. Pull over to the side of the road and stop if there is an oncoming emergency vehicle. Never drive through anything larger than a small puddle.

PREVENTION: Practicing Gas Station Safety

Static electricity can spell disaster at the fuel pump if you're not careful. As you are filling your tank, never get back inside your car no matter how cold it is because the built-up static can cause a flash fire. If you must get back inside for some reason, be certain to touch a metal part of the car away from the fill point before touching the pump. This reduces the build-up.

Never use lighters, light matches, smoke, or use a cell phone while filling your tank. Always turn your engine off and put the car in park before filling up. Never top-off or overfill your gas tank. If you are alone, be sure to lock your doors and take your keys with you if you have to leave your car to go inside the station.

To fill a container with gasoline, make sure it is approved for that use and always set it on the ground before you fill it to avoid static electricity.

If a fire starts when you are filling your tank, leave the area and call for help. Don't try to stop the pump or move the nozzle.

PREVENTION: Practicing Public Transportation Safety

Even if you own a car, you may need to take public transportation, including buses, subways, cabs, or trains. Make sure you have easy access to phone numbers, routes, and so on in your home. Be safe when using these methods of travel:

- Make sure you are indoors or have something to hold onto, like a bench or light pole, when you are waiting for a bus or taxi

- Keep your belongings secure and always touching your body

- Always keep at least one hand free to hold railings and such

- Try to ride in compartments with other people instead of alone, and try to ride in the aisle seat so that you're not blocked in

- Sit near the driver whenever possible

- Stay awake, and avoid wearing headphones because you become an easier target for theft

- Pay attention to anyone else who gets off at your stop

- Watch for slippery or uneven pavement when you board or get off

- Have your fare ready when you board the bus or subway

- When boarding or getting off a subway, be extra careful of the gap between the platform and subway door

- Wait for others to exit the bus or subway before boarding. Never try to board a bus or subway once the door starts closing

- Know where emergency buttons or cords are located

PREVENTION: Protecting Your Bicycle

Avoid making your bike an easy target for theft. Get a U-lock instead of a chain, and use it consistently. If there's nothing to attach the U-lock to, at the very least lock your bike to itself by locking the frame to the wheel. Even if you leave your bike for a few minutes, use the U-lock, and make sure you always use it with the bike's frame, not just the wheel.

Don't park your bike in public overnight. If you have an expensive bike, paint over or scratch out the brand name. Don't park your bike at the end of a bike rack because a determined thief can disassemble the rack's ends and remove your bike. Consider getting a second, low-quality bike for times when you have to leave it out overnight.

Record your bike's serial number if it has one. Engrave or otherwise add your own unique numbers or markings to the bike as well to help with identification. Get insurance for your bike; more expensive U-locks come with a guarantee that acts like insurance.

Keep a picture of your bike with your important documents.

If your bike is stolen, file a police report. Then file a claim if you have insurance.

PREVENTION: Practicing Bicycle Safety

Many bicycle injuries can be prevented. Most importantly, always wear a correctly fitted helmet that is approved by the U.S. Consumer Product Safety Commission (CPSC), the American Society for Testing and Materials, or the Snell Memorial Foundation. There should be a label on the helmet or box indicating this.

In addition, ride only at safe times in safe areas, make sure your bike is in good working order (including the brakes), and make sure it is the correct size for your body. Wear closed shoes and pants that aren't too baggy. If you ever ride at night, make sure your bike has a front light (visible from at least 500 feet ahead) and rear reflecting material (visible from at least 300 feet behind). Learn about bicycle etiquette and laws.

When riding in the city, keep the following additional safety precautions in mind:

Traffic Patterns: Never ride against traffic: Stay on the same side of the road as other vehicles. Always obey traffic signs and signals, including lane markings.

Cars: Never weave between parked cars. Don't pass a car on the right because the driver may not see you. Make eye contact with other drivers to make sure they see you.

Hand Signals: Use hand signals to tell other drivers what you intend to do. When turning left, either hand signal and use the left turn lane like other drivers or ride straight to the far crosswalk and walk your bike across like other pedestrians.

Alertness: Scan the road behind you by using a rearview mirror or looking over your shoulder without swerving. Watch for road hazards like ice, debris, sewer grates, and so on. Keep both hands ready to brake. Never ride with headphones on.

Clothing: Dress appropriately for the weather and consider wearing bright-colored clothing to make yourself more visible.

PREVENTION: Practicing Train Crossing Safety

Approaching a Crossing: Always assume there could be a train, even if you've never seen one there before. Know that a train won't be able to stop in time to avoid a collision with you. Never drive around gates or flashing red lights to try to beat an oncoming train. Over half of all collisions occur because of this. The size of the train causes an optical illusion that makes it appear farther away than it actually is. Slow down, look, and listen when you approach a train crossing. Before crossing, make sure there's room for your car to get completely across. Don't get trapped in the crossing between other vehicles.

Stalling on the Tracks: If you have a manual transmission, shift gears well ahead of or after the crossing to avoid stalling on the tracks. If you ever stall on the tracks with a train approaching, get out right away and run at an angle toward the oncoming train to better avoid flying debris. If you ever stall on the tracks without a train approaching, get out and call 911 to let them know your location so that they can contact the railroad.

Walking on the Tracks: Do not play or walk on train tracks. Never walk on railroad bridges because they aren't wide enough for you and the train if one comes. You're stuck with only two options: jump off or get hit. Never walk in railroad tunnels for the same reason.

Other: Be aware that some vehicles always stop at railway crossings. Never park your car close to train tracks. If you're at a crossing with more than one track, remember that trains can hide other trains: Make sure all of the tracks are clear before crossing.

PREVENTION: Preparing to Travel Abroad

Before traveling abroad, make sure you have a signed, up-to-date passport with the emergency information page filled out. If you don't have one, be sure to apply several months before your trip: You can do so at many post offices and other government offices. For more information on passports, visit www.travel.state.gov.

Register with the State Department so that you can be contacted if there's an emergency. The free online service

to do this can be found at www.travelregistration.state.gov.
Leave a copy of your itinerary and passport data page with
family or friends. Check your medical insurance for
overseas coverage and consider supplemental insurance if
you need it. Get any necessary additional vaccinations.
Become familiar with the country's laws.

Changing a Flat Tire

Flat tires are common, so it's useful to know how to put on
your spare tire to drive to safety. Make sure you always
have a jack, lug nut wrench (tire iron), inflated spare tire,
and WD-40 in your trunk, and be aware that spare tires
should only be driven for very short distances. Here's what
to do:

- Pull a safe distance off the side of the road, put the
  car in park, turn the engine off, and apply the
  parking brake

- Turn on your hazard lights and open your hood to
  indicate that you are stopped for repairs. You
  become more visible to other drivers, a safety
  precaution

- To prevent the car from rolling, place a heavy item
  like a large rock in front of (if facing downhill) or
  behind (if facing uphill) the diagonally opposing
  wheel. Do this even if you don't think the incline is
  very steep

- Gather your spare tire, car jack, lug nut wrench (tire
  iron), and WD-40. Gather your flashlight as well if
  it's dark

- Remove the hubcap, then loosen (but don't remove) the lug nuts that hold the wheel in place with your lug nut wrench in a counterclockwise motion. Do this in a pattern where you do one lug nut, and then the one opposite it, and then the others until they are all loosened. Spray WD-40 on any lug nuts that stick

- Slowly and carefully jack up the car. Check your owner's manual for the right spot to place the jack

- Remove the lug nuts the rest of the way and put them where they won't roll away

- Remove the flat tire and set aside

- Lift the new tire into place, checking to make sure the tire valve is facing out

- Replace the lug nuts the same way you removed them: Give each one a few clockwise turns at a time in a pattern where you never tighten adjacent lug nuts consecutively. Do one, then the opposite, and so on

- Slowly and carefully lower the jack and set aside

- Tighten the lug nuts the rest of the way

- Replace the hubcap, making sure it is secure

- Put all supplies away and drive to a garage for tire maintenance

Check the pressure on your spare tire every so often to make sure it's ready for use (temporary spares take 60 PSI and regular spares take 32 PSI). Also, be careful when you remove the flat tire: There may be sharp steel spots that can cut you.

Jump-Starting a Battery

Dead batteries are also common, so it's good to know how to jump-start your car so that you can drive instead of having to get towed to safety. Make sure you always have jumper cables in your trunk. Here's what to do:

- Put on your hazard lights and open your hood to indicate you are stopped for repairs

- Double-check your car owner's manual for any necessary information about jump-starting your car

- Find someone with a working car who is willing to help. Have them park in front of or next to your car (make sure they aren't parked illegally), put on their hazard lights, and open their hood. Make certain both cars are not actually touching each other. Also, make sure both cars are turned off with the keys pulled out

- Gather your jumper cables. Gather your flashlight as well if it's dark

- Attach the red/positive jumper cable clamp to the positive terminal (marked with a plus sign) of the helper's charged battery

- Attach the other red clamp to the positive terminal (marked with a plus sign) of your car's dead battery

- Attach the black/negative jumper cable to your car. Do it where it can ground out, like a bolt or bracket on the engine or unpainted metal part of the frame

- Attach the other black/negative jumper cable to the helper's car. Again, do it where it can ground out, like a bolt or bracket on the engine or unpainted metal part of the frame. Be careful: There may be a spark

- Try to start your car (the one with the dead battery)

- If it doesn't start, try reclamping or turning the red/positive jumper cable to the positive terminal of the helper's charged battery. Try to start your car again

- Once your car is running, remove the clamps one at a time. Start with the black/negative jumper cables and then the red/positive cables

- Allow your jump-started car to run for half an hour, driving or idling, to charge the battery

Never touch the metal ends of the jumper cables with your hands or touch them to each other. Also, never touch both battery terminals at the same time

Getting Unstuck from Snow

Make sure you are dressed warmly, take frequent breaks, and drink plenty of fluids because getting your car unstuck can be very physically demanding and time-consuming. Try to get help whenever possible.   Try one or more of the following techniques:

- Shovel around the car's tires and then shovel a path to the cleared road

- Place rock salt or ice melt under the tires and on the path to help get traction; cat litter can also work for this in a pinch

- Turn your wheels to a new direction, back up, pull forward, and try again, gently rocking your car out

- Place traction mats (available in auto parts stores) or pieces of cardboard in front of and behind the tires to help with traction

Although it can be tempting, never accelerate if your car isn't moving because it'll just get more stuck. Also, never try to drive through deep snow because you may damage your car.

Escaping a Car That Is Underwater

It's an uncommon occurrence, but you may find yourself needing to escape a sinking or underwater car in a hurry. If you can open the door and escape, do so. If you can't open the door but a window is open, use the window to escape. If neither option is available, you'll have to break a window to escape. Be aware that front windshields are made of tempered glass and aren't very breakable: You'll have better luck with side windows if you use a sharp object or a blunt object with enough force.

When you break the window, water will rush in, and you won't be able to fight against it. Instead, stay calm, hold your breath once the water gets high, release your seatbelt, and then swim out through the window.

Keep your seatbelt on until you're ready to swim out, but be ready to cut it with a tool if it won't release you. There are tools that you can buy online to attach to your key chain or keep in your vehicle that serve as emergency seatbelt cutters, the same ones used by emergency personnel.

Pets

PREVENTION: Preparing Your Pets for an Emergency

Place collars with rabies and identification tags on all of your pets. Stay current with their immunizations and veterinary visits. Keep careful track of their health records and include the records as part of your bug out bag's important documents. Also include a picture of you together with each pet as proof of ownership in an emergency.

Place *Pets Inside* stickers near your front and back doors; these notify firefighters that there are pets in the house and how many. You can get a free pet safety kit, including the stickers, from the ASPCA (American Society for the Prevention of Cruelty to Animals) website: www.aspca.org.

As for supplies, keep extra pet food stored, but not for so long that it expires or grows moldy. Keep an extra supply of your pets' regular medications as well. Have a mini bug out bag prepared for your pets that includes enough water and food for three days, any necessary medications, sanitation needs, and favorite toys. Have the following methods of transporting pets available if you must evacuate:

Dogs: Leash and collar (with muzzle?) and/or cage
Cats: Cat carrier
Birds: Travel-sized cage
Rabbits, rats, mice, lizards, and so on: Travel-sized cage or breathable pillowcase
Fish or other aquatic pets: Travel-sized tank

Set up a buddy system with reliable neighbors to care for your pets if you are away. Have other out-of-town buddies set up to care for your pets if you have to evacuate: This can of course be the same out-of-town locations you have established for yourself, like close friends or family. Many public shelters won't allow pets, so it's essential to have this buddy system set up in advance.

If for some reason you must evacuate without taking your pets, which is not recommended, make sure you leave a note on your door indicating the types and how many pets are inside. Leave plenty of food and water out, toilets open, and sinks and possibly even your bathtub filled with clean water. Open a few windows for air and leave a few lights on for visibility. If you plan ahead, you should be able to evacuate with your pets. They are likely to die, suffer injury, or get lost if they are left behind.

Protecting Yourself from an Aggressive Animal

General: Even if they look friendly or cuddly, wild animals should always be left alone. Avoid stray dogs and cats. Never try to separate fighting animals. Never leave young children alone with pets. Don't try to pet someone's dog or cat without the owner's permission.

Dogs: If you are approached by a hostile dog, stand still (don't run) then face the dog as you slowly back away. Stay very still, covering your head, if you are knocked down. Do not show fear: Dogs are more apt to bite if they know you are afraid. Avoid startling a dog. Don't touch a dog when it's eating, sleeping, caring for its young, or chewing on a toy. Keep your eyes on the dog because it's more likely to bite you when you're not looking. Don't let a dog get behind you. Don't kick at a dog. Never assume a dog won't bite, even if the owner says so.

Cats: If you hold a cat and it starts to squirm, let it go. If the cat is wagging its tail from side to side, leave it alone.

If a pet or wild animal bites you, wash the wound with soap and warm water, seek medical attention, and report the incident to the local animal control agency. You will be asked for a description of the animal and where you were bitten.

Part 5: Specific Disaster Situations

It's important to know how to prepare for and handle the most common or devastating disaster situations.

- Active Shooter
- Biological Attack
- Chemical Attack
- Civil Unrest
- Earthquake
- Explosion
- Flood
- Heat Wave
- Hurricane
- Landslide
- Nuclear Blast
- Pandemic
- Power Outage
- Radiation Attack
- Thunderstorm
- Tornado
- Tsunami
- Volcano
- Wildfire
- Winter Storm

Active Shooter

An active shooter is someone who is armed and is using deadly force against targeted or random victims. (Anywhere)

PREVENTION: Become familiar with your family's work and/or school procedures for dealing with an active shooter. Learn the locations of all exits, phones, and public address systems.

During (Shooter Inside Building):

- Immediately move to a safe location if you hear shots fired or see an armed person shooting people

- If you can't safely leave the building through an exit or window, locate a dark room and shut the door. Avoid hallways and restrooms. If you can't lock the door, barricade it with desks or other furniture. Remain silent and close to the floor

- Do not leave your location until given the all clear by police

- If you are able to exit the building, keep your hands above your head and follow any instructions given by police officers

- If you have to run across an open space like a parking lot or hallway, run in a zig-zag pattern so that you're harder to hit

- Call 911 and alert others in your vicinity once you are clear of the building or safe in a dark and locked or blocked room

- Do not interfere with police officers, even if you are wounded. Their priority will be to find the shooter before helping any wounded. Keep your hands open in plain view, and do exactly as they say

- If you come into direct contact with the shooter, use common sense: play dead, run away in a zig-zag pattern, attempt negotiation, or attempt to overcome the shooter with violence. There is no set response in this situation

During (Shooter Outside Building):

- If you hear shots fired or see an armed person shooting people outside, turn off the lights, lock the doors, and lock the windows. If you can't lock the doors, barricade them with desks or other furniture. Remain silent and close to the floor

- Do not leave your location until given the all clear by police

- Call 911 and alert others in your vicinity once you have locked or blocked the doors and windows

- If you come into direct contact with the shooter, use common sense: play dead, run away in a zig-zag pattern, attempt negotiation, or attempt to overcome the shooter with violence. There is no set response in this situation

Biological Attack

A biological attack involves the deliberate release of germs that can sicken or kill you. These germs can enter through your airways, your mouth, or an open cut on your skin. (Anywhere)

PREVENTION: Measure and precut plastic sheeting for your room/area designated for sheltering in place.

During:

- Stay informed to decide if you should evacuate or shelter in place

- Quickly evacuate if authorities give the instruction to do so, and don't return until they say it is safe

- Quickly shelter in place if authorities give instruction to do so, and don't leave your shelter until they say it is safe

- Protect your airways

- If you have symptoms that match the germ, seek medical attention

Chemical Attack

A chemical attack involves the deliberate release of toxic gases, liquids, or solids that can sicken or kill you. Symptoms often include difficulty breathing, watery eyes, and stinging skin. (Anywhere)

PREVENTION: Measure and precut plastic sheeting for your room/area designated for sheltering in place.

During:

- Stay informed to decide if you should evacuate or shelter in place

- Quickly evacuate if authorities give the instruction to do so, and don't return until they say it is safe

- Quickly shelter in place if authorities give instruction to do so, and don't leave your shelter until they say it is safe

- Protect your airways

- If you think you have chemical exposure, take off your clothes and wash right away. Seek medical attention

Civil Unrest

Civil unrest includes violent public disturbances and rioting: These can have political, racial, financial, or other causes. (Anywhere)

PREVENTION: Avoid areas where riots are known to be happening.

During:

- Stay informed to decide if you should evacuate or stay put

- Quickly evacuate if authorities give the instruction to do so, and don't return until they say it is safe

- Avoid public transportation, stopping your car, and high-traffic roads and areas as you leave the area

- If you are caught in a riot, remain calm and get indoors right away because most riots occur outdoors

- Keep doors and windows locked and stay away from them to better avoid stray bullets or rocks. Keep a low profile in an interior room

- If you cannot get indoors, move to the sidelines as inconspicuously as possible. Don't run because it draws attention

- Keep track of where the police are and avoid being hit by riot control chemicals like tear gas

Earthquake

An earthquake is the sudden shaking of the earth caused by the shifting of underground rock. (Anywhere)

PREVENTION: Make sure your home is structurally sound and repair any ceiling and wall cracks. Securely fasten all shelves to the walls, and keep heavy items on low shelves. Store toxic, flammable, and fragile items in low cabinets with latched doors. Secure your water heater to the wall and bolt it to the floor. Learn how to shut off your gas, electric, and water.

During:

- Stay informed. It is not currently possible to predict when an earthquake will happen

- Go to a safe place in your home away from windows and other glass where you are protected from falling debris

- If you are outdoors during an earthquake, avoid buildings, bridges, and power lines

- Protect your airways as needed

After: Avoid downed power lines and damaged structures.

Explosion

An explosion can have various causes, including a bomb or gas leak. (Anywhere)

PREVENTION: Learn the locations of all exits from your family's work and/or school.

During:

- Take shelter against or under a sturdy table or other piece of furniture

- Exit the building as soon as possible. Avoid elevators

- Call 911 once you are clear of the blast zone

- If you are trapped by debris after the explosion, signal for help so that rescuers can locate you. Use a flashlight, whistle, wall tapping, or other method. Avoid shouting for help, though, because you may inhale too much dust

- Avoid all unnecessary movement

- Protect your airways

After: Avoid downed power lines and damaged structures.

Flood

A flood is a large overflow of water caused by heavy rains or melting snow. (Anywhere)

PREVENTION: If you live in an area prone to flooding, make sure you have flood insurance coverage. Make sure your water heater, furnace, and electric panels are elevated off the ground. Seal and waterproof your basement walls.

During:

- Stay informed to see if you should evacuate or stay put. A flood warning means a flood is happening or will likely happen soon; a flood watch means one is possible

- Construct barriers around your home to stop floodwater

- Quickly evacuate if authorities give the instruction to do so, and don't return until they say it is safe

- If time allows, unplug electrical appliances and move them to higher levels. Also, bring in all outdoor furniture, garbage cans, and other items

- Do not drive into floodwaters, and avoid walking through moving water

After: Avoid downed power lines and damaged structures.

Heat Wave

A heat wave is an extended period of extreme heat, often including high humidity. (All but the coldest states)

PREVENTION: Make plenty of shade a part of your landscaping.

During:

- Stay informed of the Heat Index to see if you should stay indoors or in the shade

- Stay inside cool buildings, preferably air conditioned, during the hottest hours of the day

- Avoid intense outdoor activities and drink plenty of fluids (not alcoholic or caffeinated)

- Dress in light-colored, loose-fitting clothing

- Don't leave children or pets inside a parked car

Hurricane

A hurricane is a severe tropical storm with winds exceeding 75 mph. (Any coastal state)

PREVENTION: Keep all trees and plants on your property trimmed.

During:

- Stay informed to decide if you should evacuate. A hurricane warning means one is expected in your area; a watch means one is possible

- Quickly evacuate if authorities give the instruction to do so, and don't return until they say it is safe

- Prepare your home by bringing in all outdoor furniture, garbage cans, and other items. Cover all windows with wood or hurricane shutters

After: Avoid downed power lines and damaged structures.

Landslide

A landslide, also known as a mudslide, can be caused by natural disasters or human development. (Anywhere)

PREVENTION: Don't build near natural erosion alleys, drainage routes, or steep slopes. Have flexible water and gas pipe fittings that are more resistant to breaking installed by professionals.

During:

- Stay informed, though landslides often happen with little or no warning. Look for landscape changes that signal a landslide is possible, like cracked pavement or foundations

- Move away from the landslide's path as quickly as possible

- Curl into a ball, protecting your head, if you can't escape its path

After: Avoid downed power lines and damaged structures.

Nuclear Blast

A nuclear blast involves an explosion of intense heat and light that spreads radioactive material over a large area. (Anywhere)

PREVENTION: Measure and precut plastic sheeting for your room/area designated for sheltering in place. This area should be underground or in a basement, if possible.

During:

- Stay informed to decide if you should evacuate or shelter in place

- Quickly evacuate if authorities give the instruction to do so, and don't return until they say it is safe. Your best protections against radiation are minimizing your time exposed to the radiation, distancing yourself from the blast, and shielding yourself with thick materials to absorb more of the radiation

- Quickly shelter in place (below ground if possible) if authorities give instruction to do so, and don't leave your shelter until they say it is safe

- Protect your airways

- Take Potassium Iodate or Potassium Iodide if authorities give instruction to do so

- If you think you have radiation exposure, take off your clothes and wash right away. Seek medical help

Pandemic

A pandemic involves a global disease, like influenza, outbreak. (Anywhere)

PREVENTION: Make garlic a part of your diet. Allicin, an active compound found in garlic, has antibiotic properties, though research is still being done. Wash your hands frequently. Take good physical care of yourself.

During:

- Stay informed

- Stay home from work or school if you are sick

- Cover your coughs and sneezes with a tissue or your arm/sleeve

- Protect your airways as needed

Power Outage

A power outage, also called a blackout, is a loss of electricity in an area or region. (Anywhere)

PREVENTION: Locate and learn how to use the manual release lever for your garage door opener if you have one. Make emergency flashlights or other light sources easily accessible throughout your home.

During:

- Stay informed with a battery-powered or hand-crank radio to see if you should stay put

- Avoid using candles for lighting because of their extremely high fire risk

- Turn off and unplug electrical appliances except for one lamp that you can use to tell when the power is back on

- Avoid opening the refrigerator and/or freezer

- If you have room, place mostly full plastic water containers (leave at least an inch of space for the water to expand as it freezes) in your freezer and/or refrigerator. This will help keep food cold for a longer time

- Avoid travel during a power outage because traffic lights probably won't be working

Radiation Attack

A radiation attack, also called a dirty bomb, involves the use of explosives to spread radioactive materials over an area. (Anywhere)

PREVENTION: Measure and precut plastic sheeting for your room/area designated for sheltering in place. This area should be underground or in a basement, if possible.

During:

- Stay informed to see if you should evacuate or shelter in place

- Quickly evacuate if authorities give the instruction to do so, and don't return until they say it is safe. Your best protections against radiation are minimizing your time exposed to the radiation, distancing yourself from the blast, and shielding yourself with thick materials to absorb more of the radiation

- Quickly shelter in place (below ground if possible) if authorities give instruction to do so, and don't leave your shelter until they say it is safe

- Protect your airways

- Take Potassium Iodate or Potassium Iodide if authorities give instruction to do so

- If you think you have radiation exposure, take off your clothes and wash right away. Seek help

Thunderstorm

A thunderstorm is a rainstorm accompanied by lightning and thunder. (Anywhere)

PREVENTION: Remove dead trees and tree limbs that could fall and cause damage.

During:

- Stay informed to see if you should stay put. A warning means a thunderstorm has started or is about to start; a watch means one is possible

- Stay indoors as much as possible and close and shutter all windows and doors to the outside

- Secure any objects, like outdoor furniture, that could blow away

- Don't shower or bathe during a thunderstorm because the plumbing can conduct electricity

- Unplug and don't use electrical items or appliances because power surges can damage them

- Don't make calls using a corded phone because the phone line can conduct electricity (cell phones and cordless phones are fine, though)

- If you are caught outdoors, avoid water, bridges, tall trees, telephone poles, hilltops, wire fences, small metal vehicles, and large groups of people. Try to crouch in a low valley or ravine or inside a car with rolled up windows

Tornado

A tornado is a violent, rotating column of air whirling at up to 300 mph with a vortex of up to a few hundred yards diameter. (Anywhere)

During:

- Stay informed to see if you should take shelter. A tornado warning means a tornado is happening; a tornado watch means one is possible

- Quickly take shelter underground or in a basement, if possible. If neither is possible, use an interior room on the lowest floor possible

- Turn off gas, electric, and water if you have time

- Avoid windows, doors, and outside walls and stay toward the center of the room

- Avoid cars, mobile homes, and bridges. If shelter is not available, lie flat in a ditch or other low location

After: Stay clear of downed power lines and damaged structures.

Tsunami

A tsunami, also called a seismic sea wave, is an enormous ocean wave caused by an earthquake or other underground activity. It can measure over 100 feet in height and travel over 100 mph. (Any coastal state)

During:

- Stay informed to see if you should evacuate. A tsunami warning means one has already generated, a watch means one is possible and is at least 2 hours away, and an advisory means an earthquake has occurred and may generate one

- Quickly evacuate (heading inland) if authorities give the instruction to do so, and don't return until they say it is safe

- Be aware that a major drop in coastal water could indicate an approaching tsunami

After: Stay clear of downed power lines and damaged structures.

Volcano

When an active volcano erupts, it spews lava, debris, and poisonous gases that can travel for hundreds of miles. (The Pacific Northwest, Alaska, and Hawaii)

During:

- Stay informed to see if you should evacuate

- Quickly evacuate if authorities give the instruction to do so, and don't return until they say it is safe

- Protect your airways as needed

After: Stay clear of downed power lines and damaged structures.

Wildfire

A wildfire is a raging fire that spreads rapidly in areas where there are a lot of plants and trees that can easily catch fire. (Anywhere)

PREVENTION: Practice fire safety.

During:

- Stay informed to see if you should evacuate

- Quickly evacuate if authorities give the instruction to do so, and don't return until they say it is safe

- Protect your airways as needed

After: Stay clear of downed power lines and damaged structures.

Winter Storm

A winter storm includes blizzards (greater than 35 mph winds and less than 20 degree Fahrenheit temperatures), heavy snows (greater than 4 inches of snow within 12 hours or greater than 6 inches within 24 hours), ice storms, sleet storms, and snow squalls (heavy snows and high winds for a short time). (All but the warmest states)

PREVENTION: Keep snow shovels and rock salt handy. Learn how to shut off your water in case a pipe bursts. Keep your car maintained with at least a half tank of gas at all times.

During:

- Stay informed of the Wind Chill Factor to see if you should stay put. A warning means a winter storm has begun or is about to begin; a watch means one is possible

- Stay indoors as much as possible and avoid unnecessary travel

- Dress warmly and in layers, including your head and hands

- Walk carefully on icy sidewalks

After: Drink plenty of fluids (not alcoholic or caffeinated) and avoid overexerting yourself when shoveling snow. Stay clear of downed power lines. Avoid walking or standing below large icicles.

Part 6: Health Basics

Your physical and emotional states go a long way toward helping, or hindering, you during an emergency. Genetics cannot change, but lifestyle can. What are positive lifestyle choices you can make for both your body and mind?

- Physical Basics
- Emotional Basics

Physical Basics

You will have a better chance of survival if your body works for, not against, you.

PREVENTION: Avoiding Addictions

It's plain common sense: Addictions of any sort can be a liability in an emergency situation because withdrawal symptoms can be severe. Take a close look at your life and make a priority out of eliminating, or at least limiting, the following or other addictions:

Cocaine	Caffeine
Heroin	Alcohol
Crystal meth	Tobacco
Marijuana	Sugar
Prescription medications	Food
Painkillers	Online gaming
Gambling	Internet

Obviously, do not stop taking prescription medications that you need to control chronic health issues. Get professional help with breaking your addictions as needed. If you have any known addictions when an emergency occurs, include them in your planning (cigarettes in your bug out bag, extra instant coffee, etc.)

PREVENTION: Practicing Physical Fitness

You don't have to be an Olympic athlete to stand a better chance of surviving life or death situations, but physical fitness does help your odds considerably. Would you be able to run up or down flights of stairs, for example? Or lift yourself up onto a shelf?

In general, try to engage in moderate-intensity physical activities for at least 30 minutes at least 5 days a week. Or, engage in vigorous-intensity physical activities for at least 20 minutes at least 3 days a week. Moderate-intensity activities include brisk walking, dancing, swimming for fun, and biking, for example. Vigorous-intensity activities include jogging, biking uphill, doing aerobics, or swimming laps, for example.

Never begin an exercise regimen without first getting your doctor's okay, and make sure you work up gradually instead of overdoing it. Always do warm-up and cool-down activities before and after exercising.

There are five main components to physical fitness. Here are a few suggested methods for improving each one:

Cardiorespiratory: walking, swimming, biking, jogging, dancing, aerobics, tennis

Flexibility: stretching, yoga, swimming

Muscular Endurance: walking, swimming, biking, jogging, dancing

Muscular Strength: lifting weights, Pilates

Body Composition: any of the above (this simply represents the relative amounts of muscle and fat to a person's total body weight)

Here are other ways to stay physically fit:

- Get regular medical check-ups (follow your doctor's advice)

- Go to your dentist every 6 months for check-ups

- Make sure you eat a healthy diet and maintain a normal body mass index (BMI)

- Take daily vitamins or other supplements (follow your doctor's advice)

- Quit smoking if you haven't already

- Get adequate sleep (close to or more than 8 hours a night for most people)

- Limit alcohol (Men up to two drinks per day; Women up to one drink per day)

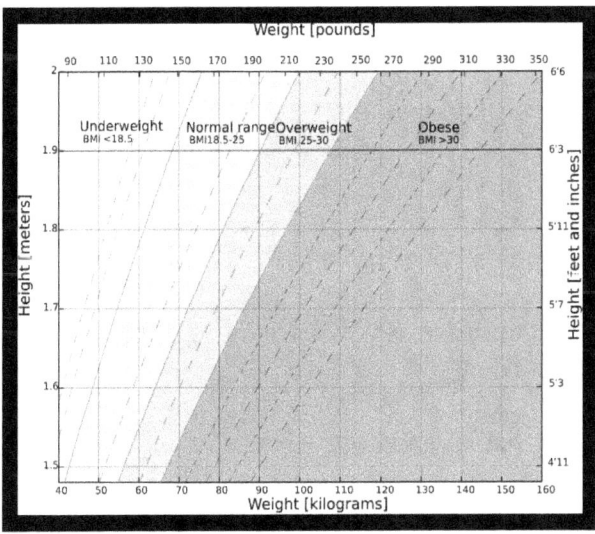

BMI Chart

Emotional Basics

Your mindset will get you further in an emergency situation than anything else.

Recognizing PTSD

PTSD stands for Post-Traumatic Stress Disorder, a not uncommon anxiety disorder caused by exposure to a traumatic event. You hear of soldiers suffering from it, but it can affect anyone: Most Americans will face at least one traumatic event in their lives, and a disaster can of course qualify as such an event.

You can get PTSD from directly being involved in the traumatic event, witnessing the trauma, or even just hearing about it. Here are some symptoms:

- Having frequent upsetting thoughts about the traumatic event

- Having recurring nightmares and/or sleep difficulties

- Having recurring flashbacks, feeling like the event is happening all over again

- Feeling acute distress when reminded of the traumatic event

- Having irritability and/or outbursts of anger

- Having difficulty concentrating

- Feeling constantly on guard

- Getting easily startled

- Feeling distant from others and losing interest in once important activities

- Avoiding conversations or thoughts about the traumatic event

- Having a hard time remembering details of the traumatic event

It's important to make a distinction between PTSD, which is long term, and Acute Stress Disorder, which is short term. Exhibiting the criteria above just after a traumatic event but then getting better within a month's time qualifies as the latter. If you or someone you know experiences either disorder, though, seek professional help.

Managing Anger

Managing your anger is an important part of getting through—and coping after—an emergency:

- Learn your personal triggers, situations or things that automatically make you angry, and take steps to avoid them

- Use humor to take the edge off your anger. Try to avoid sarcasm, though

- Learn to relax using deep breathing, visualization, and/or yoga techniques

- Explore better communication strategies, like taking time before you say the first thing that comes to mind and not jumping to conclusions

- Remind yourself that anger doesn't solve anything, but logic can. Try to remove cursing and use "I" statements in your argument repertoire

- Take a time-out: Mentally count to ten or leave the situation completely when needed

- Engage in a physical activity as a healthy outlet for your anger

- Don't hold a grudge: Forgive

- Once you feel calmer, express your anger in a controlled manner as soon as possible because to hold it in hurts you physically and emotionally

Handling Stress

An emergency will cause stress, so you must become adept at dealing with it:

- Minimize your exposure to things you find stressful. Take breaks from the stressful situation as needed and/or allowed

- Learn some deep-breathing techniques

- Change how you think to see the positive, however small, in the situation. Look at it as an opportunity to become a stronger person, for example

- Set realistic goals

- Use humor to take the edge off your stress

- Avoid "what if" thinking or dwelling on worst-case or macabre scenarios

- Avoid unnecessary arguments

- Maintain an emotional reserve to protect yourself

- Focus on health: getting close to or more than 8 hours of sleep a night, eating a balanced diet, exercising regularly, avoiding addictions, and getting relaxation time

- Share your feelings with close friends and family; don't let your emotions get bottled up

- Surround yourself with positive, cheery people

- Spend time helping others, a great distraction from your own issues

- Reward yourself with things that make you feel good

- Forgive your own mistakes and don't focus on your faults; you are not perfect. Accept the things you can't change about yourself or others

- A few times each day, do a body check for tensed muscles and let them relax

- Seek professional help as needed

Part 7: Emergency First Aid

Included here is first aid emergency information. Make sure you have access to a more thorough resource somewhere in your home, and remember that getting regular CPR/first aid training should be a priority for you and your family. Actions given below do not include the initial steps of obtaining consent (if the person is conscious) and using barriers or the final step of getting medical attention through EMS or a medical facility.

- Allergic Reaction (Anaphylaxis)
- Asthma Attack
- Bleeding Wound (Open Wound)
- Bruise (Closed Wound)
- Burn (1st, 2nd, 3rd Degree)
- Choking
- Drowning
- Eye Injury
- Fracture of Sprain
- Frostbite
- Gunshot Wound
- Head, Neck, or Back Injury
- Heart Attack
- Heat Cramps, Exhaustion, Stroke
- Hypothermia
- Insect Sting
- Internal Bleeding
- Nosebleed
- Poisoning
- Seizure
- Shock
- Stroke
- Teeth Knocked Out

Allergic Reaction (Anaphylaxis)

Signs:

Swelling, redness, difficulty breathing, coughing, wheezing, dizziness, hives, rash, itching, nausea, stomach cramps, vomiting

Actions:

Call 911. Locate the prescribed medication (epinephrine auto-injector) and verify the name, directions, and expiration date. Remove the safety cap. Inject the medication at a 90-degree angle into the person's thigh or arm and hold for 10 seconds. Give the used epinephrine auto-injector to emergency personnel.

Asthma Attack

Signs:

Coughing, wheezing, shortness of breath, rapid breathing, difficulty swallowing, sweating, chest tightness, confusion

Actions:

Locate the prescribed inhaler and verify the name, directions, and expiration date. Shake and remove the safety cap. Have the person breathe out and place their lips around the mouthpiece. Press down on the inhaler while the person inhales. Have the person hold their breath for 10 seconds and then exhale. Rinse out their mouth with water.

Bleeding Wound (Open Wound)

Signs:

Broken skin with blood coming through to varying degrees

Actions:

Cover the wound with a sterile dressing. Apply direct pressure until the bleeding stops. Cover the dressing with a bandage. If the bleeding doesn't stop, call 911, apply additional dressings and bandages, and give first aid for shock. Be aware that an open wound probably needs stitches if it's on the face, it's over half an inch long, or its edges don't fall together. Get stitches within a few hours of the injury.

Bruise (Closed Wound)

Signs:

Skin area changing color to dark red or purple, tenderness, swelling

Actions:

Apply direct pressure to the wound. Elevate the wound if it doesn't cause more pain. Apply a cold pack or ice to the wound for no longer than 20 minutes at a time.

Burn (1st, 2nd, 3rd Degree)

Signs:

Red skin, dry skin, swelling, tenderness (1st degree)

Red skin, wet skin, swelling, tenderness, blisters that weep clear fluid (2nd degree)

Black or charred skin with tissue underneath appearing white, tenderness (or relative lack of pain if the nerve endings were destroyed) (3rd degree)

Actions:

Call 911 for serious burns. Stop the burning. Cool the burn with cold running water until the pain lessens. Do not break any blisters. Cover the burn loosely with a sterile dressing. Give first aid for shock if needed.

Choking

Signs:

Inability to breathe, inability to speak, coughing, hands around throat

Actions:

Call 911 first unless you are the only responder. Follow the **First Aid: Performing the Heimlich Maneuver** section. If you are choking but are able to breathe, cough to clear your airway, then take a slow, deep breath, then give a forceful cough.

Drowning

Signs:

Swimmer flailing arms, swimming unevenly, lying facedown in water, only head with open mouth appearing above water, coughing, vomiting, pale skin, difficulty or no breathing, weak or no heartbeat, unconsciousness

Actions:

Get the person out of the water without risking drowning yourself. If the person has no pulse and is not breathing, give CPR. If they have a pulse but are not breathing, give rescue breaths. If they have a pulse and are breathing, put them in the recovery position. Call 911. Treat them for hypothermia as needed.

Eye Injury

Signs:

Eye pain, burning, redness, swelling, feeling like something is in the eye, tearing, light sensitivity, blurred vision, blindness

Actions:

For small debris, gently flush the eye with saline or purified water. For larger objects, call 911, place a sterile dressing around the object in the eye, stabilize the object with a paper cup, and bandage the area loosely without pressure to the eye. For chemicals in the eye, call 911 and flush the eye continuously until emergency personnel arrive. Be sure to flush away from the eye.

Fracture or Sprain

Signs:

Deformity, bruising, swelling, bone fragments sticking out of wound, coldness, numbness, sensation of bones grating, inability to use the affected body part, sound of snapping or popping when injury happened

Actions:

Call 911 if there's an obvious deformity or the person can't bear the weight. Check the injured body part for circulation, feeling, color, and warmth. Splint the injured body part in the position found and only if the person must be moved and it doesn't cause them more pain. Give first aid for shock as needed.

Frostbite

Signs:

Lack of feeling in the affected area, cold skin, waxy skin, discolored skin

Actions:

Get the person out of the cold. If you are close to a medical facility or if it might refreeze, do not rewarm the frostbitten area; otherwise, rewarm the area by soaking it in warm (not hot) water until color returns and the area feels warm. Do not rub the affected area or break any blisters. Bandage the area loosely with sterile dressings. If fingers or toes are affected, place sterile gauze between them to keep them separated.

Gunshot Wound

Signs:

Bleeding wound that has a point of entry (and possibly a point of exit)

Actions:

Check the area so that you don't get shot as well. Call 911. Do not move the person unless their safety is in jeopardy. If they are unconscious and not breathing, give CPR. If they are unconscious but breathing, place them in the recovery position. If they are conscious, make them sit or lie in a position that's comfortable for them. Give first aid for a bleeding wound. Give first aid for shock unless the wound is above the waist. If the gunshot wound is to the chest, seal the wound with plastic to keep air from entering the wound, which will help prevent a collapsed lung. Remove the plastic if the person starts to have trouble breathing.

Head, Neck, or Back Injury

Signs:

Complaints of neck or back pain, weak extremities, tingling extremities, intoxication, lack of alertness, involvement in a car accident or fall

Actions:

Call 911. Minimize the person's movement. Manually support the person's head as it's found with both hands. Do not move the head if it's sharply turned to one side. For minor head injuries, apply an ice pack to the injured area for no more than 20 minutes at a time. Take pain relievers as needed.

Heart Attack

Signs:

Chest pain or pressure lasting longer than 3-5 minutes or going away and coming back, chest pain that spreads to the shoulders/neck/jaw/stomach, shortness of breath, difficulty breathing, nausea, vomiting, dizziness, fainting, sweating, pale skin

Actions:

Call 911. Have the person rest and loosen any tight clothing. Assist with medication if prescribed. Give the person one aspirin (up to 325 mg) with a small amount of water (only if they aren't allergic to aspirin, on blood thinners, or have stomach ulcers or disease). Give CPR if the person's heart stops beating; use an automated external defibrillator (AED) if one is available and you're trained to do so.

Heat Cramps, Exhaustion, Stroke

Signs:

Painful leg or abdomen spasms (heat cramps)
Heavy sweating, weakness, cool skin, flushed skin, pale
skin, dizziness, headache, nausea (heat exhaustion)
Red skin, hot skin, dry or moist skin, altered consciousness,
vomiting (heat stroke)

Actions:

Move the person to a cool place. Loosen any tight clothing
and remove any sweaty clothing. Apply cool, wet towels to
their skin. Fan the person. If they are conscious, give them
small amounts of cool water to drink. Give them salty
foods like saltine crackers if they can handle it. If they lose
consciousness, refuse water, or vomit, call 911 and place
them on their side. Use ice or cold packs on their wrists,
ankles, groin, neck, and armpits.

Hypothermia

Signs:

Shivering, numbness, weakness, altered consciousness, glassy stare, unconsciousness

Actions:

Move the person to a warm place. Give CPR if they are unconscious or not breathing. Remove their wet clothing. Dry them and warm them in blankets or dry clothing. If they are conscious, give them warm liquids (no caffeine or alcohol). Never warm the person too quickly by immersing them in warm water because it may cause dangerous heart rhythms.

Insect Sting

Signs:

A stinger embedded in the skin, tenderness, possibly signs of allergic reaction

Actions:

Remove the stinger with tweezers (avoid the venom sac) or by scraping away with your fingernail. Wash the area with soap and warm water. Cover the area. Apply a cold pack. Watch the person for signs of allergic reaction.

Internal Bleeding

Signs:

Tenderness, bruised areas, hard areas, rapid and weak pulse, coughing up blood, vomiting blood, pale skin, moist skin, thirst, confusion, fainting, drowsiness, unconsciousness

Actions:

Call 911. Give first aid for shock. Give CPR if the person becomes unconscious or stops breathing.

Nosebleed

Signs:

Blood coming out the nose to varying degrees

Actions:

Have the person sit down and lean slightly forward. Pinch the nostrils together for about 10 minutes. Apply an ice pack to the bridge of the nose. If bleeding doesn't stop, apply pressure to the upper lip just beneath the nose. Call 911 if the person loses consciousness or the bleeding doesn't stop. Lay them on their side to allow blood to drain from their nose.

Poisoning

Signs:

Difficulty breathing, chest pain, abdominal pain, sweating, nausea, diarrhea, vomiting, seizure, headache, dizziness, irregular pupil size, altered consciousness, tearing eyes, irregular skin color

Actions:

Call 911 if the person is unconscious or not breathing; call the National Poison Control Center and follow the advice given if they are conscious. Try to find out the type of poison, how much was taken, when it was taken, and how it entered the body. Lay them on their left side to keep their windpipe clear. Never give them anything to eat or drink unless directed by the National Poison Control Center. If the poison was inhaled, move the person to fresh air first and avoid inhaling the fumes yourself.

Seizure

Signs:

Falling down, bodily convulsions, stiffening, eyelid fluttering, eyes rolling up, twitching movements, confusion, speech difficulty, drooling, teeth clenching, sweating, altered consciousness, unconsciousness

Actions:

Remove nearby objects. Protect the person's head with a towel or clothing beneath it. Never restrain them or place anything in their mouth. Note how long the seizure lasts. Call 911 if they are pregnant, are diabetic, are unconscious or not breathing, have injured themselves, have never had a seizure before, have a seizure for longer than 5 minutes, or have a second seizure. Place them in the recovery position after the seizure.

Shock

Signs:

Rapid breathing and pulse, pale skin, cool skin, altered consciousness, confusion, irritability, restlessness, thirst, nausea

Actions:

Call 911. Keep the person from getting chilled by covering them with a blanket. Elevate their legs 8 to 12 inches if you don't suspect a head, neck, back, hip, or leg injury. Don't give them anything to eat or drink. If they vomit, roll them onto their side.

Stroke

Signs:

Weakness on one side of the face, slurred speech, trouble speaking, numbness or weakness in one arm

Actions:

Call 911. Note the time the signs were first observed.

Teeth Knocked Out

Signs:

Displaced teeth

Actions:

Rinse out the person's mouth with cold water. Have them bite down on a rolled sterile dressing in the space left by the missing teeth. Pick up the teeth by the crown (not the root), rinse off if dirty (but don't remove any tissue fragments), and place in a glass of milk. Get the person to a dentist within 30-60 minutes.

Part 8: Closing

Attitude is everything: This is discussed before closing with a list of websites for further information.

- The Right Attitude
- Additional Information

The Right Attitude

Doomsday and end of the world scenarios fill our consciousness and perhaps make it just a little bit harder to function day to day. There is so much we don't know, after all, that we can only guess. What are some of the worst-case scenarios?

Asteroid impact
Rogue Black Hole
Giant solar flare
Global pandemic
Earth's magnetic field reversing
Runaway global warming
Erupting volcano harming the atmosphere
Biotech disaster
Collapsing ecosystems
Nanotechnology disaster
Environmental toxins
Large-scale or global war
Artificial intelligence taking over technology

It's a numbers game: Perhaps our number will come up some day, and humanity will lose big. In the meantime, don't forget the importance of hoping for the best.

Perhaps the psychology behind disaster preparedness involves wanting to feel some sense of control over an all too uncontrollable world, but then again that may be one of the healthiest outlets for this control urge. Extremists out there can take anything too far, but it's absolutely healthy to be prepared for power outages, blizzards, civil unrest, and other emergencies that Mother Nature and humanity can throw at us. In the world we live in, anything less is extremely unhealthy.

Even if one or more of these doomsday scenarios play out, we have our hope and knowledge to see us through. Don't spend life dwelling on future possibilities, spend it cherishing the present realities.

Additional Information

The following are a few websites for more information on disaster preparedness and related issues:

www.ready.gov
Department of Homeland Security

www.fema.gov
Federal Emergency Management Agency

www.redcross.org
American Red Cross

www.ohsa.gov
Occupational Safety and Health Administration

www.epa.org
Environmental Protection Agency

www.cdc.gov
Centers for Disease Control and Prevention

www.fda.gov
U.S. Food and Drug Administration

www.nws.noaa.gov
National Weather Service

www.nod.org
National Organization on Disability

www.ncd.gov
National Council on Disability

www.apsp.org
Association of Pool and Spa Professionals

www.donotcall.gov
Federal Do Not Call Registry

www.homefoodsafety.org
American Dietetic Association

www.nimh.nih.gov
National Institute of Mental Health

www.avma.org/disaster
American Veterinary Medical Association